Introduction to Accounting

Lynda Street

Apart from any fair dealing for the purpose of research or private study, or criticism or review, as permitted under the Copyright, Designs and Patents Act 1988, this publication may only be reproduced, stored or transmitted, in any form or by any means, with the prior permission in writing of the publisher, or in the case of reprographic reproduction in accordance with the terms and licences issued by the Copyright Licencing Agency. Enquiries concerning reproduction outside those terms should be addressed to the publishers' agents at the undermentioned address:

BANKERS BOOKS LIMITED
c/o The Chartered Institute of Bankers
90 Bishopsgate
London EC2N 4AS

CIB Publications are published by The Chartered Institute of Bankers, a non-profit making registered educational charity, and are distributed exclusively by Bankers Books Limited which is a wholly owned subsidiary of the Chartered Institute of Bankers.

The Chartered Institute of Bankers believes that the sources of information upon which the book is based are reliable and has made every effort to ensure the complete accuracy of the text. However, neither CIB, the author nor any contributor can accept any legal responsibility whatsoever for consequences that may arise from errors or omissions or any opinion or advice given.

Copyright © Chartered Institute of Bankers 1996

ISBN 0-85297-404-3

First published in Great Britain by the Chartered Institute of Bankers (London)

This student edition is published in Sri Lanka by the Institute of Bankers of Sri Lanka (IBSL) in May 2001 under the licence granted by the Chartered Institute of Bankers (CIB) in terms of the memorandum of Agreement signed between the CIB and IBSL.

Contents

Introduction

UNIT 1   Balance Sheet

UNIT 2   Trading Profit and Loss Account

UNIT 3   Double Entry BookKeeping, Ledger, Personal and Nominal Accounts, Trial Balance

UNIT 4   Accruals, Prepayments, Bad Debts and Provision for Bad Debts

UNIT 5   Depreciation

UNIT 6   Partnership Accounts

UNIT 7   Company Accounts

UNIT 8   Incomplete Records

UNIT 9   Cash Flow Statements

UNIT 10   Costing

UNIT 11   Budget Forecasts and Cash Flow Forecasts Part I

UNIT 12   Cash Flow Forecasts Part II

UNIT 13   Concepts and Conventions of Accounting

UNIT 14   Bank Reconciliation

UNIT 15   Ratio Analysis

UNIT 16   Valuation of Stock, Work-in-Progress and Manufacturing Accounts

UNIT 17   Written Answer Questions

UNIT 18   Past Paper Questions – Numerical

Answers to self-assessment questions

Introduction

> **Objectives**
>
> By the end of this introduction you will be able to:
> - understand the aims of this course, its structure, its recommended reading, and the principles behind activities, questions and assignments which are set
> - understand the examination structure.

1 Aims of the course

1.1 Accounting is more than the recording and reporting of transactions for periodic financial statements. The nature and purpose of accounting is very wide, being used both internally by the organisation and outside the organisation by many others. The external users include shareholders, bankers, lenders, investment analysts and government departments. Accounts prepared for income tax purposes or to comply with the Companies Act 1985 may not necessarily be suitable for the purposes of every other user. What you come to appreciate is the different ways in which the accounting data may be analysed to aid users in their decision-making. The data is tailored to the needs of the organisation and, where appropriate, to other users.

1.2 The course is not designed to train you as a bookkeeper, because the emphasis is not on detailed entries in ledgers but on the later stages of preparing accounts and reports. However, it will be beneficial for you to have a good working knowledge of double entry bookkeeping because it is the foundation on which accounts are based. Many weaknesses in students' understanding of accounts can be traced to a lack of knowledge of the fundamentals.

1.3 If you have not studied accountancy prior to undertaking this course, you should concentrate initially on the recording of transactions and how they are classified within the accounting system. This will involve you in understanding the jargon which is used so frequently in accountancy.

2 Course structure

2.1 Introduction to Accounting is a core subject of business study. The course is designed to take you through the theory and practice of recording and preparing accounts for all types of profit-making organisations and non-profit-making organisations.

2.2 At the appropriate stages you will learn the concepts and conventions of accounting and how those have been incorporated into standard practice in an attempt to provide uniformity of presentation. However, if possible, frequent use should be made of the recommended textbook and in particular the questions at the end of each chapter. There are, also, plenty of exercises for you to do with the answers in the back of the book.

3 Recommended textbook

3.1 While there is no essential textbook for this course, we do recommend that you read:

3.2 *Introduction to Accounting for the Banking Certificate* by Howard Mellett and Dick Edwards, published by CIB.
ISBN: 0.85297.274.1.

4 Assignments

4.1 The purpose of this section is to define the different kinds of tests and activities included in the course.

- **Self-assessment questions**. These are short questions designed to test your knowledge of what you have studied so far. There are self-assessment test questions at the end of each Unit. Answers are also given as feedback.

- **Activities**. These will help you develop your understanding as you work through the lessons. They are included periodically in the lessons together with appropriate feedback. Activities are signalled in the text with the following icons:

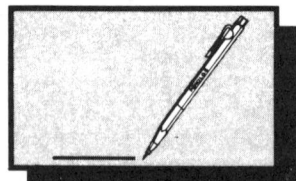

As practice is essential in accounting to ensure that you are fully able to answer questions within the appropriate time and accurately, a special Unit has been devoted to the more usual types of questions at the end of your course in addition to the above features.

5 Plan of study

You should study the Units in order. The 'Reading' refers to the recommended textbook which you may wish to study in parallel with the course.

		Reading Chs
Unit 1	Balance sheet	1/2
Unit 2	Trading profit and loss account	3
Unit 3	Double entry bookkeeping, ledger, Personal and Nominal Accounts, Trial Balance	4
Unit 4	Accruals, Prepayments, Bad Debts and Provision for Bad Debts	5
Unit 5	Depreciation	5
Unit 6	Partnership Accounts	7
Unit 7	Company Accounts	8/9
Unit 8	Incomplete Records	3
Unit 9	Cash Flow Statements	
Unit 10	Costing	10
Unit 11	Budget Forecasts and Cash Flow Forecasts Part I	10
Unit 12	Cash Flow Forecasts Part II	10
Unit 13	Concepts and Conventions of Accounting	6/9
Unit 14	Bank Reconciliation	4
Unit 15	Ratio Analysis	11
Unit 16	Valuation of Stock, Work-in-Progress and Manufacturing Accounts	5/6
Unit 17	Written Answer Questions	
Unit 18	Past Paper Questions – Numerical	

6 Examination details

When you sit the CIB exam, the paper will be set in three sections:

- *Section A* consists of one compulsory question on the preparation of final accounts from the trial balance. At least 10 marks must be attained in section A to gain an overall pass. (20 marks).

- *Section B* will consist of 10 questions, each carrying 4 marks. The questions will take the form of notes and or calculations. Candidates answer 5 or 10 questions of their own choice. (20 or 40 marks).

- *Section C* will consist of 4 questions, each worth 20 marks. This section could contain questions which are a mixture/combination of calculations, interpretations, analysis and discussion. Candidates answer 2 or 3 questions (40 or 60 marks).

Candidates select combinations of questions to cover a total of 100 marks.

Questions will not be asked on any new legislation, etc., until it is in operation. Although candidates will be expected to be aware of developments up to the date of the examination, *detailed* knowledge will not be required of legislation, etc. coming into operation less than six months prior to the examination.

Candidates may use silent, *non-programmable* calculators in this examination.

The examiner insists that all headings are written in full and not abbreviated and that all such headings are underlined. If you follow this advice then you will not be throwing away marks, all of which are needed to pass the examination.

Unit 1

Balance Sheet

> **Objectives**
>
> By the end of this Unit you will be able to:
> - define a balance sheet
> - draw up a balance sheet
> - explain how additions/deletions to a balance sheet affect the final outcome
> - explain the difference between fixed and current assets
> - explain the difference between long-term and current liabilities
> - experiment with movements in the balance sheet to see how they affect the assets and liabilities.

1 Introduction

1.1 Management of any business needs to know if it is making a profit or a loss and if it can meet its future commitments. To assess this, management needs to know what the business owns, what money is owed and how much it owes to others. This information is drawn together into a balance sheet to show the financial position of a business at a particular point in time. We will look at the balance sheet in this first Unit of Introduction to Accounting.

2 The balance sheet

2.1 The balance sheet shows how the business is using its resources.

2.2 The balance sheet is an equation and as such it must balance. It is divided into two halves: the assets and the liabilities.

3 Assets and liabilities

The assets

3.1 The assets represent the resources of the business. These consist of the premises, equipment, stock, debtors, bank account, cash, etc. Some of these terms will be explained in more detail later on.

3.2 All assets are given a monetary value on the balance sheet.

The liabilities

3.3 The liabilities are made up of the capital, the amount of money put into the business by the owner(s), and other commitments which have to be repaid, such as loans and creditors.

3.4 All liabilities have a monetary value in the balance sheet.

3.5 Because the balance sheet is an equation, the assets must equal the liabilities. This equation is often expressed as:

Assets = Capital + Liabilities

3.6 The assets are the resources of the business and the liabilities are its commitments.

4 How the balance sheet is presented

4.1 The balance sheet can be presented in two formats: horizontal or vertical. Here we concentrate on the horizontal style. The vertical style is looked at later in this Unit.

4.2 The balance sheet is always headed as follows:

[Name of the firm]
Balance sheet as at [date of the accounts]

4.3 This is expressed 'as at date' because the balance sheet reflects a snapshot of the business at that time. If you drew the accounts up at a later date the balances would be different because the firm had continued trading – goods would have been bought and sold, debts created and some repaid.

4.4 The following balance sheet shows a business started and £20,000 deposited at the bank.

A Trader
Balance sheet as at 31 December 19XX

Assets	£	Liabilities	£
Bank	20,000	Capital	20,000
	20,000		20,000

5 Building a balance sheet

5.1 Using the previous example, if the owner buys premises on the same day for £10,000 paid by cheque, the balance sheet would look like this:

A Trader
Balance sheet as at 31 December 19XX

	£		£
Assets		*Liabilities*	
Premises	10,000	Capital	20,000
Bank	10,000		
	20,000		20,000

5.2 The balance sheet still balances at £20,000, but what has changed is the distribution of the assets, as £10,000 was drawn from the bank account to pay for the premises.

5.3 To continue with this example, the trader buys stock so that trading can begin, so the balance sheet now looks like this:

A Trader
Balance sheet at 31 December 19XX

	£		£
Assets		*Liabilities*	
Premises	10,000	Capital	20,000
Stock	5,000		
Bank	5,000		
	20,000		20,000

5.4 Again there is a redistribution of the assets as the stock of £5,000 is **bought** using the funds in the bank account.

6 Creditors and debtors

Creditors

6.1 Take the same situation, but instead of paying for the stock the trader takes it on credit. That is, a liability has been created. The cost of the stock is owed to a creditor. Thus, the balance sheet looks like this:

A Trader
Balance sheet as at 31 December 19XX

	£		£
Assets		*Liabilities*	
Premises	10,000	Capital	20,000
Stock	5,000	Creditors	5,000
Bank	10,000		
	25,000		25,000

6.2 The final figure of £25,000 has changed from £20,000 because a liability of £5,000 has been created.

6.3 Remind yourself of some of the terminology we have used so far by completing the following activity.

Student Activity 1

(a) Define a liability.

(b) Define an asset.

(c) State the balance sheet equation.

Feedback

6.4 You should have remembered that:

(a) A liability is a commitment of the firm, which must at some point be repaid.

(b) An asset represents a resource available to a company, such as premises or debtors.

(c) The balance sheet equation is:

Assets = Capital + Liabilities.

6.5 Now do the following activity to check your understanding of the balance sheet presentation.

Student Activity 2

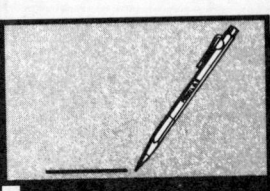

Draw up a balance sheet for 'Your Business' as at 1 January 19XX from the following information:

Capital	30,000
Premises	20,000
Stock	20,000 bought on credit
Bank Account	10,000

Refer back to the previous example if you have any problems.

Feedback

6.6 Your balance sheet should look like this:

Your Business
Balance sheet as at 1 January 19XX

	£		£
Assets		*Liabilities*	
Premises	20,000	Capital	30,000
Stock	20,000	Creditors	20,000
Bank	10,000		
	50,000		50,000

Debtors

6.7 As well as buying goods on credit the firm can also sell goods on credit. The amounts outstanding for goods sold on credit is referred to as 'debtors'. The prudent businessperson will ensure that these funds are received before the commitment to repay the creditors falls due. Debtors appear as an asset on the balance sheet.

6.8 We'll continue to use the example of A Trader. A Trader sells half the stock on credit. Remember, so far no goods have been bought from the firm. The balance sheet now looks like this:

A Trader
Balance sheet as at 31 December 19XX

	£		£
Assets		*Liabilities*	
Premises	10,000	Capital	20,000
Stock	2,500	Creditors	5,000
Debtors	2,500		
Bank	10,000		
	25,000		25,000

6.9 If a further £500 of goods are sold for cash and no replacements bought, the final balancing figure will be the same but two figures will change:

- stock will be reduced by £500

- the bank account will be increased by £500.

6.10 These figures will appear on the asset side of the balance sheet and the new balance sheet after these changes will appear as follows:

A Trader
Balance sheet as at 31 December 19XX

Assets	£	Liabilities	£
Premises	10,000	Capital	20,000
Stock	2,000	Creditors	5,000
Debtors	2,500		
Bank	10,500		
	25,000		25,000

7 Fixed and current assets

Fixed assets

7.1 These are long-term assets that the business needs to enable it to function; they are not primarily intended for resale in the ordinary course of business. At some stage in the future these assets may be sold or scrapped as new ones are acquired. These assets consist of freehold premises, long leasehold premises, equipment and vehicles, etc. From this list you will appreciate why at some stage these fixed assets will need to be replaced, but as this is not their prime function in the business they are therefore called fixed assets.

7.2 The fixed assets are presented in the balance sheet in the order of their expected life span, with the one with the longest life first and so on. So this will be presented as follows:

Fixed assets
Premises   (longest life)
Equipment
Vehicles   (shortest life)

Current assets

7.3 Current assets are those that have a relatively short lifespan. These are the assets used in the ordinary course of business, and they include stock, debtors, bank accounts in credit and cash. A current asset is cash or assets that can easily be turned into cash. Again, they are presented in a set order, with the most difficult asset to turn into cash being placed at the top, working through to the most liquid asset – cash – holding bottom position. This will be presented in the balance sheet as follows:

Current assets
Stock   (least liquid)
Debtors
Bank accounts
Cash   (most liquid)

8 Capital, long-term liabilities and current liabilities

Capital

8.1 Capital is always the first item on the liabilities side of the balance sheet. The capital will be increased or decreased by the net profit or loss calculated in the trading profit and loss account (see Unit 2). Any drawings made by the owner(s) will be deducted from this figure. (Drawings are profits taken out of the business by the owner.)

Long-term liabilities

8.2 The next section on the liabilities side of the balance sheet is headed long-term liabilities. These are items such as long-term loans and mortgages which are not expected to be repaid in the near future.

Current liabilities

8.3 These are liabilities which have to be repaid in the near future, such as creditors and the bank overdraft.

8.4 The liabilities side of the balance sheet would be presented as follows:

Capital
Plus net profit or minus net loss
Minus drawings

Long-term liabilities
Bank loan

Current liabilities
Creditors
Bank overdraft

8.5 You will see that once again the most permanent liabilities appear first and then in descending order, with bank overdraft being last as repayment is on demand.

9 The working capital cycle

9.1 Another way of looking at current assets and current liabilities is to say that the most common ones (stock, debtors cash/bank and creditors) are used directly in the process of buying and selling goods. I buy stock either for cash or on credit, sell it to debtors who eventually pay me cash, with which I buy more stock or pay off my creditors, etc.

9.2 This is known as 'the working capital cycle' and is very important in accounting.

Figure 1: Working capital cycle

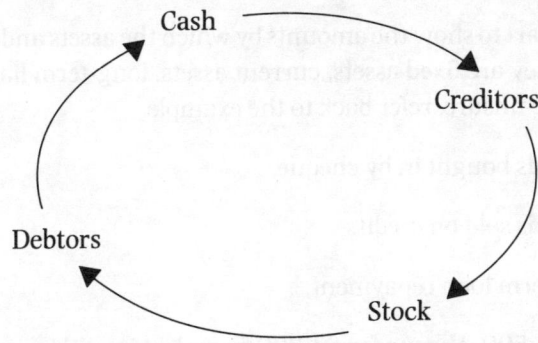

9.3 This will be covered in more detail later on.

10 Movement of assets and liabilities

10.1 This section expands on the movement of assets and liabilities in the balance sheet.

10.2 Remembering that the balance sheet must balance, it follows that any change to one item in the balance sheet must be matched by a change to an item on the other side. We saw this earlier on when, for example, an increase in stock was matched by a similar decrease in cash, both on the assets side, an increase in stock bought on credit would, however, be balanced by an increase in the liability 'creditors'. Remember the change will always balance out. Some other examples are:

		Assets	*Liabilities*
(a)	Stock bought for cash	Increase in stock Decrease in cash	–
(b)	Stock bought on credit	Increase stock	Increase creditors
(c)	Equipment bought by cheque	Increase fixed assets Decrease bank account	
(d)	Equipment bought by long-term bank loan	Increase fixed assets created	Increase long-term liability bank loan

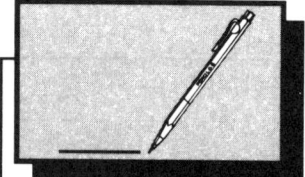

Student Activity 3

Prepare a similar chart to show the amounts by which the assets and liabilities change. Indicate whether they are fixed assets, current assets, long-term liabilities or current liabilities. If you are unsure, refer back to the example.

(a) £500 of goods bought in by cheque.

(b) £100 of goods sold on credit.

(c) £500 long-term loan repayment.

(d) Overdraft £2,500, cheque for £3,000 from debtor paid in.

(e) Premises bought with a 25–year mortgage – cost £60,000, mortgage £55,000.

(f) Equipment bought, £10,000 by cheque with the balance of £20,000 by a 5-year bank loan.

Feedback

10.3 Your chart should include the various transactions as follows:

		Assets £	Liabilities £
(a)	*Current assets*		
	Stock increased	500	
	Bank account decreased	-500	
(b)	*Current assets*		
	Stock decreased	-100	
	Debtors increased	100	
(c)	*Current assets*		
	Bank account reduced	-500	
	Long-term liabilities		
	Loan account reduced	-500	
(d)	*Current liabilities*		
	Bank overdraft repaid		-2,500
	Current assets		
	Bank account credit balance	500	
	Debtors decreased	-3,000	
(e)	*Fixed assets*		
	Premises increased or new	60,000	
	Current assets		
	Bank account reduced	-5,000	
	Long-term liabilities		
	Mortgage increased or new		55,000
(f)	*Fixed assets*		
	Equipment increased or new	30,000	
	Current assets		
	Bank account reduced	-10,000	
	Long-term liabilities		
	Bank loan increased or new		20,000

10.4 This exercise should have given you a better understanding of the balance sheet.

10.5 Now prepare a balance sheet from given information.

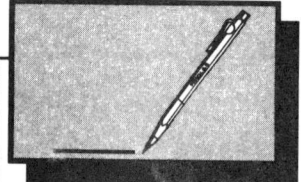

Student Activity 4

Draw up a balance sheet for B Trader as at 31 December 19XX, from the following information:

Capital	15,000
Premises	20,000
Equipment	5,000
Vehicles	2,500
Long-term loan	15,000
Creditors	1,000
Stock	2,500
Debtors	2,250
Bank overdraft	1,500
Cash	250

Tip: If you have trouble remembering whether some items are assets or liabilities and therefore have difficulty in balancing the balance sheet, add all the totals up and divide by two. This will give you the balancing figure for both sides.

Feedback

10.6 Once you have decided on which items are assets and liabilities, you should have been able to include them in the appropriate format for a balance sheet as below.

B Trader
Balance sheet as at 31 December 19XX

	£		£
Fixed assets			
Premises	20,000	Capital	15,000
Equipment	5,000		
Vehicles	2,500	*Long-term liabilities*	
	27,500	Loan	15,000
Current assets		*Current liabilities*	
Stock	2,500	Creditors	1,000
Debtors	2,250	Bank overdraft	1,500
Cash	250		
	32,500		32,500

10.7 Now let us take this balance sheet a little further and see what effect the following changes will have on the balance sheet:

(a) £500 of stock sold on credit.

(b) £1,000 of stock bought on credit.

(c) Equipment costing £3,000 bought by increasing the long-term loan.

(d) £1,000 of goods sold for cash which was deposited in the bank account.

10.8 Think about the likely effects and perhaps make pencilled notes next to the balance sheet above before looking at the result below.

B Trader
Balance sheet as at 31 December 19XX

	£		£
Fixed assets			
Premises	20,000	Capital	15,000
Equipment	8,000		
Vehicles	2,500	*Long-term liabilities*	
	30,500	Loan	18,000
Current assets		*Current liabilities*	
Stock	2,000	Creditors	2,000
Debtors	2,750	Bank overdraft	500
Cash	250		
	35,500		35,500

11 Balance sheet presentation – vertical style

11.1 The balance sheets we have looked at so far have been presented in horizontal format. These days it is more common to present them in vertical format. We showed you the horizontal format first as it is easier for a learner to see what is going on when it is presented in this way.

11.2 The difference in the format is, quite simply, that the assets are moved above the capital and liabilities in the vertical format. By rearranging the order of components, we are able to gain a better picture of the company's position. You will see how, by studying the following balance sheet.

11.3 From now on, we will present the information in the format shown below:

Balance sheet as at 31 December 19XX

	£	£
Fixed assets		
Premises		xx
Equipment		xx
		xx
Current assets		
Stock		xx
Debtors	xx	
Bank		xx
Cash		xx
	xx	
Current liabilities		
Creditors	−xx	
Working capital		+xx
		*xx
Capital		xx
Net profit		xx
		xx
Less drawings		xx
		*xx

*These lines must balance.

11.4 To make this more realistic, we'll include some figures on this:

Capital	10,000
Net profit	5,000
Drawings	1,000
Premises	13,000
Stock	3,000
Debtors	500
Bank	500
Creditors	3,000

11.5 This now provides us with a vertical balance sheet as follows:

Balance sheet as at 31 December 19XX

	£	£
Fixed assets		
Premises		13,000
Current assets		
Stock	3,000	
Debtors	500	
Bank	500	
	4,000	
Current liabilities		
Creditors	3,000	
Working capital		1,000
		14,000
Capital		10,000
Net profit		5,000
		15,000
Drawings		1,000
		14,000

11.6 This vertical form of presentation is preferred as it indicates the company's working capital (i.e. the difference between current assets and current liabilities).

WC = CA–CL

11.7 Working capital examines the company's liquidity position, and its ability to meet short-term debts as they fall due.

12 Summary

12.1 In this Unit, you have seen that balance sheets are prepared according to the following equations:

Assets = Capital + Liabilities (Horizontal Format)
Capital = Assets − Liabilities (Vertical Format)

12.2 The assets are the firm's resources, items and money owned by the business and owed to it, and the liabilities are its commitments.

12.3 The balance sheet is a snapshot of the business as at a particular date. It can be presented in two formats: horizontal or vertical. You now know how the balance sheet is drawn up, and how assets and liabilities appear on the balance sheet and change it as they are created.

12.4 You have had the opportunity to draw up some balance sheets and make them balance!

12.5 You now know the difference between long-term liabilities, current liabilities, fixed assets and current assets. You also know the order in which these appear in the balance sheet together with the capital. You have revised and developed the effects of movements in the balance sheet.

Self-assessment questions

1. What is shown by a balance sheet?

2. Explain the difference between current assets and fixed assets.

3. Explain the difference between long-term liabilities and current liabilities.

4. Define the following terms:

    (a) Debtors

    (b) Creditors

    (c) Drawings

    (d) Capital

5. Remember the balance sheet equation (presented slightly differently here):

    Assets – Liabilities = Capital.

    Complete the table with appropriate figures so that the balance sheet equation holds true for each line.

	Assets	Liabilities	Capital
(a)	50,000		10,000
(b)		65,000	15,000
(c)	60,000	15,000	

6. Put these current assets in the order you would expect to find them in a balance sheet:

    Debtors, Cash, Stock, Bank

7. Define and give an example of a current liability.

8. What is the correct heading for a balance sheet?

9. As the debtors represent money owing to the business, do they appear as assets or liabilities?

10 Draw up the balance sheet, in vertical form, for 'Your Business' as at 31 December 19XX from the following:

Capital	15,000
Net profit	3,000
Drawings	1,500
Premises	10,000
Equipment	2,000
Creditors	2,000
Stock	4,000
Debtors	2,000
Bank	500

Unit 2

Trading Profit and Loss Account

Objectives

By the end of this Unit you will be able to:
- draw up a trading, profit and loss account
- explain the distinction between capital and revenue expenditure
- make entries for carriage in and out and returns in and out.

1 Introduction

1.1 Having looked at the balance sheet which gives us an idea of the assets and liabilities in a business, we will now turn to the performance of the business and the statement which shows success from trading. This is the financial account which shows if the firm has made a profit or a loss. It is divided into two parts; the trading account gives the gross profit, and the profit and loss account gives the net profit. These accounts appear together usually in one document called the trading profit and loss account.

2 The gross profit

2.1 The gross profit, which gives an indication of the success generated by the business from buying and selling goods, is calculated by finding the difference between the sales and the cost of these sales (i.e. the purchase price less any adjustments). The gross profit is commonly expressed as:

Gross profit = Sales - cost of goods sold

Putting some figures to this equation, it looks like this:

	£
Sales	1,000
Cost of goods sold	700
Gross profit	300

2.2 This is a simple example that assumes that all the stock bought has been sold. In reality there would be more stock bought so that the business could continue trading.

2.3   Let us then add opening and closing stock figures. The previous example with these figures would be as follows:

	£	£
Sales:		1,000
Opening stock	200	
Add purchases	<u>700</u>	
	900	
Less closing stock	<u>250</u>	
Cost of goods sold		650
Gross profit		<u>350</u>

2.4   The trading profit and loss account is always headed up with the name of the firm and the period the accounts cover. It would be presented as follows:

A Trader
Trading profit and loss account for the year ended 31 December 19XX

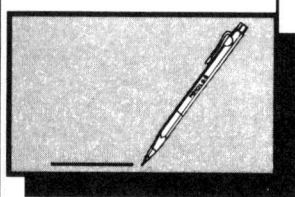

Student Activity 1

Draw up the trading account and calculate the gross profit from the following information for A Trader.

	£
Purchases	800
Opening stock	550
Closing stock	450
Sales	1,200

Feedback

2.5 Your trading profit and loss account should look like this:

A Trader
Trading profit and loss account for the year ended 31 December 19XX

	£	£
Sales		1,200
Opening stock	550	
Add purchases	800	
	1,350	
Less closing stock	450	
Cost of goods sold		900
Gross profit		300

2.6 Now that you can calculate the gross profit it is time to look at the net profit.

3 The net profit

3.1 The net profit is the sum of the business expenses – e.g. rent, rates, heating, lighting, salaries – deducted from the gross profit. So, we find that:

Gross profit - Operating expenses = Net profit

3.2 Here is an example of a trading profit and loss account:

A Trader
Trading profit and loss account for the year ended 31 December 19XX

	£	£
Sales		10,000
Opening stock	3,500	
Add purchases	5,000	
	8,500	
Less closing stock	4,000	
Cost of goods sold		4,500
Gross profit		5,500
Less expenses		
Heat and light	1,200	
Salaries	2,500	
Rates	500	
Telephone	200	
		4,400
Net profit		1,100

3.3 So in this example the gross profit was £5,500 and the net profit £1,100.

Student Activity 2

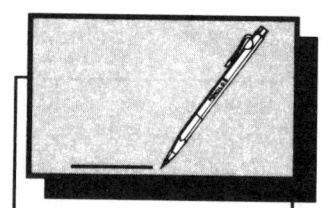

Now it is your turn to draw up a trading profit and loss account for 'Your Business' for the year ended 31 December 19XX from the following information:

	£
Opening stock	10,000
Closing stock	8,500
Purchases	10,000
Sales	17,500
Heating and lighting	1,500
Salaries	3,000
Rates	1,000
Telephone and postage	250

Feedback

3.4 Your trading profit and loss account should look like this:

Your Business
Trading profit and loss account for the year ended 31 December 19XX

	£	£
Sales		17,500
Opening stock	10,000	
Add purchases	10,000	
	20,000	
Less closing stock	8,500	
Cost of goods sold		11,500
Gross profit		6,000
Less expenses		
Heat and light	1,500	
Salaries	3,000	
Rates	1,000	
Telephone and postage	250	
		5,750
Net profit		250

3.5 The net profit is £250 and this will be added to the 'capital' figure in the balance sheet. So you can now complete the accounts by drawing up the balance sheet for 'Your Business'.

3.6 The following exercise adds to your revision of Unit 1 and illustrates how the trading profit and loss account links with the balance sheet.

Student Activity 3

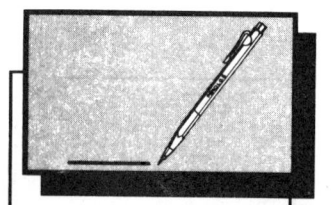

Use your calculations above and the information below to draw up the balance sheet for Your Business in vertical form.

	£	
Capital	5,000	
Long-term bank loan	10,000	
Creditors	5,000	
Premises	10,000	
Stock	8,500	(i.e. the closing stock)
Debtors	3,000	
Bank O/D	1,250	

Feedback

Your Business
Balance sheet as at 31 December 19XX

	£	£	£
Fixed assets			10,000
Current assets:			
Stock		8,500	
Debtors		3,000	
		11,500	
Current liabilities:			
Creditors	5,000		
Bank o/d	1,250		
		6,250	
Working capital			5,250
			15,250
Less: Long–term liabilities			
Loan			10,000
			5,250
Capital			5,000
Add net profit			250
			5,250

4 Capital expenditure

4.1 Capital expenditure relates to expenditure on fixed assets.

4.2 You will remember from your earlier work that fixed assets are long-term assets which the business needs to function; they are not primarily intended for sale in the ordinary course of business.

4.3 So if the business needs, say, some new equipment, this purchase is capital expenditure. If there were a purchase which increased the value of an existing fixed asset, then this too is capital expenditure.

5 How capital expenditure is treated in the accounts

5.1 As already stated, a purchase of a fixed asset or an increase in an existing fixed asset is capital expenditure; it is because of this that its treatment in the accounts is only reflected in the balance sheet. The cost of the purchase increases the fixed asset figure in the balance sheet. The corresponding entry could be a reduction in cash in the bank account or the creation of a liability or a combination of both.

5.2 For example, if I bought premises for £100,000 and paid £50,000 cash and £50,000 by way of mortgage, this would reduce my bank balance by £50,000 (asset) but increase my liabilities (mortgage) by £50,000.

5.3 An addition to the fixed assets is to be used for several years by the business, to help it make a profit. So if it were charged in the profit and loss account it would be against one year's profit or loss which is not realistic as the net profit would be understated or the net loss exaggerated. What happens is that, with certain fixed assets, depreciation is charged against the gross profit in the profit and loss account over the expected life of the asset. This will be explained in detail in Unit 5.

6 Revenue expenditure

6.1 Revenue expenditure is the expenditure that is both incurred in the normal course of business and does not add any value to the fixed assets. An example of this could be the purchase of stationery and postage stamps.

7 How revenue expenditure is treated in the accounts

7.1 It is because revenue expenditure does not add any value to the fixed assets that it is charged to the profit and loss account. It is realistic that this expenditure be reflected against this account because in the main it has been bought to be used during the accounting period.

7.2 Sometimes the expenditure is, in effect, a split between both capital and revenue expenditure, such as a repair to a building. In such a case the costs must be split between capital (balance sheet) and revenue (profit and loss account) expenditure as accurately as possible.

7.3 For example, if I added an extension to my factory, this would be an increase in the existing fixed asset value of my factory in my balance sheet. Compare this with painting the factory. Although it might make it look prettier, it would add nothing to the actual value of the property and would therefore appear as an expense in my profit and loss account. If I did both, it would be split into the balance sheet and profit and loss account.

8 Carriage inwards and carriage outwards

8.1 **Carriage inwards** is the cost of transport into the firm (i.e. the cost of getting the goods into the firm).

8.2 **Carriage outwards** is the cost of transport out of the firm to the customer.

9 How carriage is dealt with in the accounts

9.1 **Carriage inwards** is added to the purchases in the trading account. This gives a realistic figure for the purchases because the carriage inwards is an expense directly related to the purchase of the stock.

9.2 **Carriage outwards** is directly related to the expenses incurred in selling the goods. As such, it is charged to the profit and loss account.

9.3 The following trading, profit and loss account illustrates how entries for carriage inwards and carriage outwards are included in the accounts.

B Trader
Trading profit and loss account for the year ended 30 June 19XX

	£	£	£
Sales			20,000
Opening stock		5,500	
Add purchases	8,000		
Add carriage inwards	350		
	8,350		
		13,850	
Less closing stock		6,900	
Cost of goods sold			6,950
Gross profit			13,050
Less expenses			
Heating		500	
Lighting		150	
Wages		2,000	
Postage and telephone		250	
Carriage outwards		550	
			3,450
Net profit			9,600

10 Returns inwards and returns outwards

10.1 **Returns inwards**, as their name suggests, are goods that have been returned to the firm by its customers.

10.2 **Returns outwards** are goods that are returned by the firm from whence they were purchased.

11 How returns are dealt with in the accounts

11.1 Returns inwards are goods returned to the firm, and so they are deducted from the sales figure in the trading account.

11.2 Returns outwards are goods returned by the firm to its supplier, and so they are deducted from the purchases figures.

Student Activity 4

From the following information draw up the trading profit and loss account and balance sheet for C Trader for the year ended 31 December 19XX.

	£
Capital	25,000
Premises	50,000
Equipment	18,000
Vehicles	7,500
Debtors	5,000
Closing stock	15,000
Bank balance	2,000
Long-term bank loan	25,000
Creditors	10,000
Sales	25,000
Purchases	8,000
Opening stock	12,500
Returns inwards	200
Returns outwards	2,500
Carriage inwards	750
Carriage outwards	500
Heating	2,000
Lighting	450
Rates	2,000
Salaries	6,500
Drawings	5,000
Cash	100
Mortgage	33,000

Note: This is an extensive exercise. At this stage accuracy is more important than speed, so take your time to complete the financial statements. A methodical approach is essential.

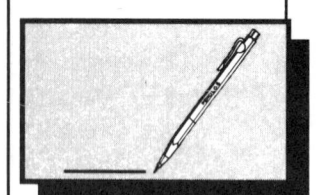

Feedback

11.3 Your trading profit and loss account should agree with this:

C Trader
Trading profit and loss account for the year ended 31 December 19XX

	£	£	£
Sales			25,000
Less returns inwards			200
			24,800
Opening stock		12,500	
Add purchases	8,000		
Less returns outwards	2,500		
	5,500		
Add carriage inwards	750		
		6,250	
		18,250	
Less closing stock		15,000	
Cost of goods sold			3,750
Gross profit			21,050
Less expenses:			
Carriage outwards		500	
Heating		2,000	
Lighting		450	
Rates		2,000	
Salaries		6,500	
			11,450
Net profit			9,600

11.4 Your balance sheet should agree with this one:

C Trader
Balance sheet as at 31 December 19XX

	£	£	£
Fixed assets			
Premises			50,000
Equipment			18,000
Motor vehicles			<u>7,500</u>
			75,500
Current assets			
Stock	15,000		
Debtors	5,000		
Bank	2,000		
Cash	<u>100</u>		
		22,100	
Current liabilities			
Creditors		<u>10,000</u>	
			<u>12,100</u>
			87,600
Less: Long-term liabilities			
Mortgage		33,000	
Bank loan		<u>25,000</u>	58,000
			<u>29,600</u>
Capital		25,000	
Add net profit		<u>9,600</u>	
		34,600	
Less drawings		<u>5,000</u>	
			<u>29,600</u>

12 Summary

12.1 In this Unit you have learned how to calculate gross profit and net profit by preparing a trading, profit and loss account. You have also seen how to deal with carriage and returns and various revenue expenses and income in the statement.

12.2 You have also had some practice in drawing up quite lengthy trading, profit and loss accounts and balance sheets from a list of receipts, expenses, assets and liabilities, so that you are able to distinguish between items which appear in the different financial statements. You have seen that the distinction between capital and revenue expenditure is an important aspect to consider when preparing these statements.

12.3 Make sure that you have mastered this area before proceeding to Unit 3, because final accounts (trading and profit and loss accounts and the balance sheet) are very important in your examination as well as your work.

Self-assessment questions

1. What is a trading account?

2. What is a profit and loss account?

3. How is a trading profit and loss account headed and how does this differ from a balance sheet?

4. (a) What is the gross profit?

   (b) What is the net profit?

   (c) To what item in the balance sheet is the net profit or loss added to or deducted from?

5. Write, in your own words, the answers to the following questions:

   (a) What is capital expenditure?

   (b) What is revenue expenditure?

6. Where are capital and revenue expenditure shown in the final accounts and why?

7. Explain what is meant by sales and purchases returns.

8. Calculate the gross profit from these figures:

Sales	£100,000
Purchases	£66,000
Purchase returns	£5,000
Opening stock	£12,000
Closing stock	£16,000

9. When preparing the trading, profit and loss account, how would you deal with the following:

   (a) carriage outwards

   (b) carriage inwards?

10   Calculate the net profit from the following figures:

Closing stock	£8,000
Sales	£200,000
Purchases	£90,000
Opening stock	£10,000
Returns inwards	£800
Returns outwards	£1,000
Carriage inwards	£600
Carriage outwards	£400
Heating and lighting	£1,200
Rent and rates	£2,400
Salaries	£9,000

Unit 3

Double Entry Bookkeeping, Ledger, Personal and Nominal Accounts, Trial Balance

Objectives

By the end of this Unit you will be able to:

- **explain the concept of double entry bookkeeping and describe how it is used**
- **draw up ledger, personal and nominal accounts**
- **complete a trial balance**
- **distinguish between purchases, sales and stock**
- **complete a set of books from a list of transactions.**

1 Introduction

1.1 Having looked at the final accounts we will now turn to the records that are used to prepare these final accounts and which underlie accounting statements generally. These records are kept using double entry principles and ledger accounts.

2 Double entry bookkeeping

2.1 The concept of double entry bookkeeping is shown by the equations you have already met when looking at the balance sheet:

Assets = Capital + Liabilities
Capital = Assets - Liabilities

2.2 If one side moves there must be some corresponding movement(s) to ensure that the equation balances. You completed some exercises in Unit 1 on what happens when there are movements in the balance sheet.

Student Activity 1

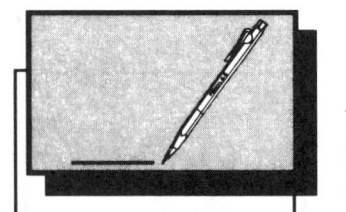

To refresh your memory, complete the following exercise by identifying the appropriate assets and liabilities concerned and whether they increase or decrease.

                                                             Asset   *Liability*

(a)   Buy goods on credit

(b)   Sell goods for cash

(c)   Sell goods on credit

(d)   Buy equipment by cheque

(e)   Buy goods for cash

(f)   Collect cheque from debtor

Feedback

2.3 You should have identified the following transactions.

	Asset	Liability
(a)	Increase stock	Increase creditors
(b)	Decrease stock Increase cash	–
(c)	Decrease stock Increase debtors	–
(d)	Increase fixed asset equipment Decrease bank account	–
(e)	Increase stock Decrease cash	–
(f)	Decrease debtors Increase bank account	–

2.4 In double entry bookkeeping there is a dual effect: an event takes place and there must be a corresponding event(s) (e.g. if in (f) the payment by the debtor had been part cash, part cheque, these two together would equal the corresponding decrease in the debtors). Now that you understand the principle of double entry bookkeeping we will look at how it is recorded.

3 Ledger accounts

3.1 Double entry bookkeeping is a record of transactions and an individual record is kept for each of the assets and liabilities. This record is known as an account. So an entry in one account, following through the principle, must have a corresponding entry in another account.

3.2 The complete set of these accounts kept by a firm is referred to as its ledger. It is therefore a collective term for all these individual accounts. This term is also sometimes used to describe a group of accounts such as the personal or nominal ledgers which we will look at later.

3.3 Now lets see how these accounts are presented.

An account

| Debit | Credit |
| Side | Side |

3.4 The format is often referred to as a T account because the rules make it look like a T.

3.5 The rules for working out if the entry is to appear on the debit or credit side are:

(i)   If the asset is increased, the account is debited.

(ii) If the asset is decreased, the account is credited.

(iii) If the liability is increased, the account is credited.

(iv) If the liability is decreased, the account is debited.

3.6 Let us put these rules to work. If goods are bought on credit then the two accounts would be as follows:

Dr	**Stock a/c**	**Cr**
	Creditor	

Dr	**Creditors a/c**	**Cr**
	Stock	

3.7 Note that the name of the corresponding account is written in the account.

3.8 Remember the entries must balance the equation; the stock account is debited and the creditors account is credited. If we put a figure to this of 100 they would be as follows:

Stock a/c

Creditor	100	

Creditors a/c

	Stock	100

3.9 The next entry is added to the account, so that a running record is kept of each account throughout the accounting period.

3.10 The amount of detail recorded in the account must be sufficient to identify the amounts owed and due, for financial statements to be drawn up, for the correct amounts to be paid and receipts checked.

3.11 The cash account will be used for all transactions for cash. The drawing or paying in of cheques will be recorded in the bank account.

3.12 To remember which account to debit and which to credit, use the following rule: debit value in and credit value out. Value is used here instead of Cash because cash is not always involved. For example, if I buy goods on credit I debit value in (Purchases) and credit value out (Creditor I owe him money).

Student Activity 2

Draw up and complete the accounts for the following entries:

(a) Buy goods on credit 500.

(b) Sell goods for cash 100.

(c) Sell goods on credit 200.

(d) Debtor repays 50 by cheque.

(e) Goods bought by cheque 300.

(f) Creditor repaid 250 in cash.

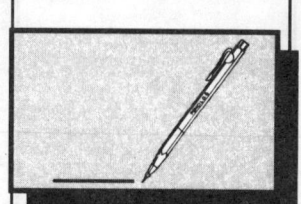

Feedback

Stock a/c

		Dr				Cr	
(a)	Creditor		500	(b)	Cash		100
(e)	Bank a/c		300	(c)	Debtor		200

Creditors a/c

		Dr				Cr	
(f)	Cash		250	(a)	Stock		500

Cash a/c

		Dr				Cr	
(b)	Stock		100	(f)	Creditor		250

Bank a/c

		Dr				Cr	
(d)	Debtor		50	(e)	Stock		300

Debtors a/c

		Dr				Cr	
(c)	Stock		200	(d)	Bank		50

3.13 Remember that if one account is debited the other must be credited so that the double entry is complete and the books balance.

3.14 These accounts must balance. At the end of the accounting period the difference of the two sides is entered to balance. The balancing figure is then carried forward to the next period. An example is given below.

Debtors a/c

Dr				Cr		
10/7/XX	Stock	100	31/8/XX	Cash		50
			31/12/XX	Balance c/d		50
		100				100
1/1/X1	Balance b/d	50				

3.15 In other words, we are carrying forward the net balance on each account.

3.16 It is important that each transaction is dated, and this is shown on the left-hand side of the detail.

3.17 The number of individual accounts maintained will depend on what is required and what is realistic. A fleet of vans might be owned and rather than have individual records for each vans petrol, repairs and general running costs, it might be more appropriate to have a vans expenses account, or some other variation.

4 Personal and nominal accounts

4.1 The ledger may well be split into personal and nominal accounts.

4.2 Personal accounts are held to record the transactions between the firm and outsiders, like creditors and debtors. So far we have generalised and recorded the transactions in one general account called creditors and debtors, but in reality you must know who these individuals or firms are to make and receive payment. So individual accounts are held for all parties. So if you have debtors of X, Y and Z and your creditors are A, B and C then six accounts will be held: A, B, C, X, Y and Z.

4.3 The debtors ledger is called the sales ledger

4.4 The creditors ledger is called the purchase ledger.

4.5 Nominal accounts refer to the record of transaction which in turn go to the trading profit and loss account. The sort of accounts this would include are rent, rates, wages and salaries, purchases and sales.

5 Trial balance

5.1 Double entry bookkeeping requires a credit for each debit so that the accounts balance. You have already worked through this procedure. The trial balance brings together these figures so that they can be formulated into the trading profit and loss Account and balance sheet. From the T accounts, all balanced off, you bring any outstanding balances to the trial account. Two examples are shown below.

A Debtor a/c

Dr			Cr		
1/6/XX	Stock	300	1/9/XX	Bank a/c	300
		300			300

B Debtor a/c

Dr			Cr		
1/10/XX	Stock	300	1/12/XX	Bank a/c	200
			31/12/XX	Balance c/d	100
		300			300
1/1/XX	Balance c/d	100			

5.2   In this example A Debtor would not be brought into the trial balance because the debt has been repaid in full. B Debtor still owes 100 so this figure is taken to the trial balance.

5.3   The trial balance is a summary of the balances remaining in the various ledgers, with the debits on one side and the credits on the other. The trial balance should always balance it checks the arithmetical accuracy of the books. It is used to prepare a trading profit and loss account.

5.4   Obviously, if the trial balance does not balance, there must be one or more mistakes. However, there are a number of errors which will not affect the totals of trial balance. These are:

- **Error of principle**: an entry made in the wrong account, e.g. wages debited to purchases.

- **Omission**: a transaction has been completely omitted.

- **Compensatory**: errors two or more errors which cancel each other out.

- **Error in original entry**: an incorrect figure may be used as the basis of the double entry record.

- **Duplication**: details entered twice.

Student Activity 3

Draw up the T accounts and the trial balance from the following transactions (there are no balances brought down from the previous period):

(a) Stock 500 bought from A. Brown with cash.

(b) Stock 300 sold on credit to F. Smith.

(c) Debtor F. Smith repays 50 by cheque.

(d) Stock 1,000 bought on credit from A. Brown.

(e) Creditor A. Brown paid 100 by cheque.

(f) Stock 300 sold to J. Jones on credit.

(g) F. Smith repays 250 by cheque.

(h) Rent paid 100 by cheque.

You will need separate sheets of paper to complete this activity.

Feedback

5.5 Your accounts and trial balance should look like these:

Stock a/c

Dr				Cr			
(a)	A. Brown		500	(b)	F. Smith		300
(d)	A. Brown		1,000	(f)	J. Jones		300
					Balance c/d		900
			1,500				1,500
	Balance b/d		900				

Cash a/c

Dr			Cr		
Balance c/d		500	(a)	A. Brown	500
		500			500
				Balance b/d	500

F. Smith a/c

Dr			Cr		
(b)	Stock	300	(c)	Bank a/c	50
			(g)	Bank a/c	250
		300			300

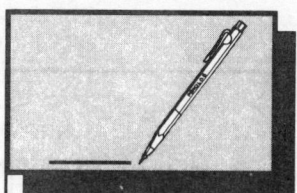

Bank a/c

Dr			Cr		
(c)	F. Smith	50	(e)	A. Brown	100
(g)	F. Smith	250	(h)	Rent	100
				Balance c/d	100
		300			300
	Balance c/d	100			

A. Brown a/c

Dr			Cr		
(e)	Bank A/c	100	(d)	Stock	1,000
(d)	Balance c/d	900			
		1,000			1,000
				Balance b/d	900

J. Jones a/c

Dr			Cr		
(f)	Stock	300		Balance c/d	300
		300			300
	Balance b/d	300			

Rent a/c

Dr			Cr		
(h)	Bank a/c	100		Balance c/d	100
		100			100
	Balance b/d	100			

Trial balance as at 31 December 19XX

	Dr	Cr
Stock	900	
Cash		500
Bank a/c	100	
A. Brown a/c		900
J. Jones a/c	300	
Rent a/c	100	
	1,400	1,400

5.5 This is only a small portion of the accounts needed to draw up a trial balance. Obviously, there would be other transactions, for, as it stands, our cash account is 500 short. This is because no previous balances were brought forward and in reality they would be. However, as long as you were able to draw up the accounts and get your trial balance to balance in this case, you have mastered this procedure.

6 Purchases, sales and stock

6.1 So far we have looked at buying and selling stock on a single account called stock, except when used in the trading, profit and loss account, when it has been broken down into purchases and sales. Why is this so? Consider the following:

- I buy stock for 500 and sell it for 1,000; a profit of 500 (sales less purchases).

- However, this assumes that I sold all the stock I bought. What if the storekeeper told me there was in fact 100 of that stock still left unsold? What is my profit now? It must be the cost of my original stock (500) less the stock I have left (100) = 400, deducted from my sales (1,000 - 400) = 600. So my profit figure depends on the closing stock figure.

- It therefore follows that since my closing stock this year will be my opening stock next year, both opening and closing stock will need to be taken into account when deciding what my real gross profit is.

6.2 Let us assume the opening stock in the example above was 300. What is my profit?

6.3 First of all I need to find the actual cost of the goods I sold during the year. This can be found as follows:

	£
I started with opening stock	300
I bought goods during the year (purchases)	500
So the total goods available for sale was	800
But at the end of the year I was left with closing stock	100
So the true cost of my goods sold was	700
Deduct it from my sales and my profit is	300

6.4 Set out in accounting fashion, the trading account looks like this:

Trading a/c

	Dr	Cr
Sales		1,000
Opening stock	300	
Add purchases	500	
	800	
Less closing stock	100	
Cost of goods sold		700
Gross profit		300

11

7 Bookkeeping a worked example

7.1 This effectively completes the basic theory of bookkeeping, so it is probably a good time to pause and reflect on what you have learnt so far. To look, as it were, at the whole picture.

- First of all a company starts with some **capital**.

- It then acquires some **assets** and possibly other **liabilities**.

- These assets and liabilities are recorded in ledgers in this case **personal ledgers**, which are records of the day-to-day business of a firm (e.g. premises, debtors, stock).

- When a company starts trading, it continues to use the ledgers to record its day-to-day transactions (purchases, sales, rent, rates, etc.). These all form part of the profit-making side of the business and are entered in the **nominal ledger**.

- At the end of a trading period these ledgers are balanced off and agreed (a **trial balance**).

- Each account is then used for a different purpose; some accounts are transferred to the trading account (e.g. sales, purchases, stock returns in and returns out) to determine gross profit; some are transferred to the profit and loss account to determine net profit.

- At this stage we have condensed all our nominal accounts into one figure, the net profit or loss.

- What is left is either capital or personal accounts (e.g. creditors, debtors, premises, motor vehicles) and will of course be used next year, so we compile a balance sheet to see how we are placed at the beginning of our next accounting year. Then the bookkeeping begins all over again.

7.2 Look at the following full example before attempting to prepare accounts yourself.

Example

7.3 The following balance sheet shows J. Smith's financial position on 31 December 19X1. The numbers against each entry can be used to trace its place in the bookkeeping.

J. Smith Balance sheet of as at 31 December 19X1

Fixed assets
Premises	3,000	(3)
Motor cars	<u>1,000</u>	(4)
	4,000	

Current assets
Debtor (B. White)	1,000	(5)
Stock	250	(6)
Bank	<u>1,750</u>	(7)
	3,000	

Current liabilities
Creditor (A. Jones)	<u>2,000</u>	(2)
	1,000	
	<u>5,000</u>	
Capital	<u>5,000</u>	(1)

7.3 During the next accounting period (31 January 19X2) the following transactions took place. (For simplicity dates have been omitted but bear in mind you would normally be expected to put these in.)

- (8) & (9)   • Buys goods for 450, pays by cheque.
- (10) & (11)   • Sells goods for 1,000, receives cheque.
- (12) & (13)   • Pays rent 500 by cheque.
- (14) & (15)   • Pays rates 250 by cheque.
- (16) & (17)   • Buys goods for 2,000 on credit from A. Jones.
- (18) & (19)   • Receives cheque from debtor (B. White) for 500.
- (20) & (21)   • Pays A. Jones 250 by cheque.
- (22) & (23)   • Sells goods for 3,000, receives cheque.

7.4 The value of stock at the end of this period is 1,000.

Required:

7.5 Enter up these transactions in the books of J. Smith, balance off the ledgers, take out a trial balance and prepare a trading, profit and loss account and a balance sheet as at 31 January 19X2.
(*Note*: It is not really necessary to balance off single items.)

Capital a/c

	(1)	Balance b/d	5,000
		(from balance sheet)	

Premises a/c

(3)	Balance b/d	3,000			

Creditor (A. Jones) a/c

(20)	Bank	250	(2)	Balance b/d	2,000
	Balance c/d	3,750	(17)	Sales	2,000
		4,000			4,000
				Balance b/d	3,750

Motor car a/c

(4)	Balance b/d	1,000			

Debtor (B. White) a/c

(5)	Balance b/d	1,000	(19)	Bank	500
				Balance c/d	500
		1,000			1,000
	Balance b/d	500			

Stock a/c

(6)	Balance b/d	250			

Bank a/c

(7)	Balance b/d	1,750	(9)	Purchases	450
(11)	Sales	1,000	(13)	Rent	500
(18)	B. White	500	(15)	Rates	250
(23)	Sales	3,000	(21)	A. Jones	250
				Balance c/d	4,800
		6,250			6,250
	Balance b/d	4,800			

Purchases a/c

(8)	Bank	450		Balance c/d	2,450
(16)	A. Jones	2,000			
		2,450			2,450
	Balance b/d	2,450			

Sales a/c

	Balance c/d	4,000	(10)	Bank	1,000
			(22)	Bank	3,000
		4,000			4,000
	Balance b/d	4,000			

Rent a/c

(12)	Bank	500

Rates a/c

(14)	Bank	250

7.6 Note 1: The letters on the left of the trial balance denote whether the figure is transferred to trading account (T), the profit and loss account (P), or the balance sheet (B). This is a good tip to follow when doing exercises from the trial balance.

7.7 Note 2: The letters on the right match the actual transfers to the trading profit and loss account and the balance sheet.

Trial balance as at 31 January 19X2

		Dr	Cr	
B	Capital		5,000	(n)
B	A. Jones (creditor)		3,750	(i)
B	Premises	3,000		(j)
B	Motor Cars	1,000		(k)
B	B. White (debtor)	500		(l)
B	Stock (opening)	250		(b)
B	Bank	4,800		(m)
T	Purchases	2,450		(c)
T	Sales		4,000	(a)
P	Rent	500		(e)
P	Rates	250		(f)
		12,750	12,750	

J. Smith
Trading, profit and loss account for the month ended 31 January 19X2

	£	£
Sales		4,000 (a)
Opening stock	250 (b)	
Add purchases	2,450 (c)	
	2,700	
Less closing stock	1,000 (d)	
Cost of goods sold		1,700
Gross profit		2,300
Less expenses:		
Rent	500 (e)	
Rates	250 (f)	
		750
Net profit		1,550 (g)

J. Smith
Balance sheet of as at 31 January 19X2

Fixed assets			
Premises			3,000 (j)
Motor cars			1,000 (k)
			4,000
Current assets			
Stock		1,000 (h)	
Debtors		500 (l)	
Bank		4,800 (m)	
		6,300	
Current liabilities			
Creditors		3,750 (i)	
			2,550
			6,550
Capital			5,000 (n)
Add net profit			1,550 (g)
			6,550

7.8 You may need to go through this a few times to get it clear in your mind. Now its your turn! Work each part separately do not attempt to do all parts at once. Complete the following activity on separate sheets of paper.

Student Activity 4

John Brown began the year 19X2 with the following balances:

Capital	12,000
Motor vehicles	3,000
Bank	6,800
Cash	200
Creditors	2,000
Debtors	2,000
Stock	2,000

(a) Draw up John Brown's balance sheet on that day and open accounts for each item.

The following entries appeared in his books during the year:

- Purchased stock for 3,000 by cheque
- Sold stock for 5,000 to A. Debtor
- Paid rent 1,000 by cheque
- Paid petrol bill 100 by cash
- Received cash 1,000 from A. Debtor
- Paid A. Creditor 1,500 by cheque
- Bought more stock 1,000 for cash
- Sold stock for 5,000 to A. Debtor
- Paid rates by cheque 300

(b) Enter the above transactions in the books of John Brown which you have already opened. Open new accounts as necessary.

(c) balance off the accounts and take out a trial balance.

You are now told that closing stock is valued at 1,000.

(d) Draw up a trading, profit and loss Account and a balance sheet.

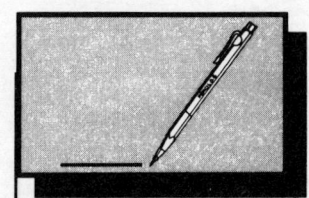

Feedback

Capital a/c

		Balance b/d	12,000

Motor vehicles a/c

Balance b/d	3,000		

Bank a/c

Balance b/d	6,800	Purchases	3,000
		Rent	1,000
		A. Creditor	1,500
		Rates	300
		Balance c/d	1,000
	6,800		6,800
Balance b/d	1,000		

Cash a/c

Balance b/d	200	Petrol	100
A. Debtor	1,000	Purchases	1,000
		Balance c/d	100
	1,200		1,200
Balance b/d	100		

Creditors a/c

Bank	1,500	Balance b/d	2,000
Balance c/d	500		
	2,000		2,000
		Balance b/d	500

Debtors a/c

Balance b/d	2,000	Cash	1,000
Sales	5,000	Balance c/d	11,000
Sales	5,000		
	12,000		12,000
Balance b/d	11,000		

Purchases a/c

Bank	3,000	Balance c/d	4,000
Cash	1,000		
	4,000		4,000
Balance b/d	4,000		

Sales a/c

Balance c/d	10,000	A. Debtor	5,000
		A. Debtor	5,000
	10,000		10,000
		Balance b/d	10,000

Rent a/c

Bank	1,000

Rates a/c

Bank	300

Petrol a/c

Cash	100

Stock a/c

Opening balance b/d	2,000

Trial balance as at 31 December 19X3

	Dr £	Cr £
Capital		12,000
Motor vehicles	3,000	
Bank	1,000	
Cash	100	
Creditor		500
Debtor	11,000	
Purchases	4,000	
Sales		10,000
Rent	1,000	
Rates	300	
Petrol	100	
Stock	2,000	
	22,500	22,500

John Brown
Trading, profit and loss account for year ended 31 December 19X3

	£	£
Sales		10,000
Opening stock	2,000	
Add Purchases	4,000	
	6,000	
Less Closing stock	1,000	
Cost of goods sold		5,000
Gross profit		5,000
Less expenses:		
Rent	1,000	
Rates	300	
Petrol	100	
		1,400
Net profit		3,600

John Brown
Balance sheet as at 31 December 19X3

	£	£
Fixed assets		
Motor vehicles		3,000
Current assets		
Stock	1,000	
Debtors	11,000	
Bank	1,000	
Cash	100	
	13,100	
Less current liabilities		
Creditors	500	
		12,600
		15,600
Capital		12,000
Net profit		3,600
		15,600

8 Drawings

8.1 Sometimes an owner of the business may take some goods (i.e. stock) for their own use. To account for this you will need to:

Dr Drawings
Cr Purchases

8.2 This will reduce the purchases figure in the trading account, and increase the drawings figure in the balance sheet.

9 Summary

9.1 In this Unit you have seen how to enter transactions into a set of books, to balance off those accounts and to take out a trial balance of those accounts.

9.2 In addition you have seen how this relates to previous Units by progressing from the trial balance to the trading, profit and loss account and finally to producing a closing balance sheet.

9.3 You have also seen how goods taken for the owners own use are accounted for.

9.4 At this stage you should take stock of your progress so far. Do not continue unless you feel you have fully grasped the concepts of bookkeeping.

Self-assessment questions

1. Complete the following by identifying the ledger accounts involved for each transaction:

   Transaction   Debit   Credit

   (a) Bought car for cash

   (b) Sold goods for cash

   (c) Paid wages by cheque

   (d) Bought goods from G. Jones

2. Explain the principle of double entry bookkeeping.

3. What is a personal account? What is a nominal account?

4. Identify whether an account has debited or credited entries in each of the following examples:

   (a) An asset is increased.

   (b) An asset is decreased.

   (c) A liability is decreased.

5. Draw up ledger accounts for the following transactions:

   (a) Goods bought on credit £400

   (b) Creditor repaid £300 cash.

6. What is a trial balance?

7. Which of the following items are debit entries and which are credit entries in a trial balance?

   (a) Assets.

   (b) Liabilities.

   (c) Income.

   (d) Expenses.

8. What is an error of principle?

9. What is an error of omission?

10. How should drawings of stock be treated in the accounts?

Unit 4

Accruals, Prepayments, Bad Debts and Provision for Bad Debts

Objectives

At the end of this Unit you will be able to:
- **define accruals, prepayments and bad debts**
- **make provisions for accruals, prepayments and bad debts.**

1 Introduction

1.1 When the trial balance is drawn up, you know that it contains the balances in the various ledger accounts. Income and expenses are then used to prepare the trading, profit and loss account and any remaining accounts with an outstanding balance are brought together into the balance sheet.

1.2 However, there are usually a number of matters at the balance sheet date which have yet to be resolved. Customers have been sold goods on credit and have not yet paid; the business has yet to pay salaries although employees are owed two or three weeks' money for work done since the last pay-day. We will look at such problems and some of the ways in which the accounting system deals with such problems in this Unit.

2 Accruals

2.1 In the preparation for accounts so far, we have assumed that expenses such a rent, rates and electricity have been paid to cover the exact accounting period. In reality however, some services will have been used in expense incurred that have not been paid for.

2.2 An example is the use of the telephone, which is paid for retrospectively. An organisation will have had the benefit of the telephone for a time before the end of the accounting period and the bill may not have been presented for payment. (If a bill has been presented for payment, but not yet paid, this will appear in the accounts as a creditor.) The cost of the telephone must be reflected in the accounts, however, as it has been incurred during this period. That is, it reflects an expense that must be applied in the profit and loss account so that a true position is reported.

2.3 In the accounts an accrual must be raised to reflect any such benefit. If the account is set, for example, leasing of equipment at 1,500 a quarter you will know the exact amount to include as an accrual. The amount may need to be divided to reflect the period outstanding. For example, if you paid 1,500 a quarter to lease equipment and you have used the equipment for two months of that quarter, the accrual would be 1,000.

2.4 If a bill has not yet been received, an assessment of the amount can be made by referring to previous bills where they exist. For example, if you have used the telephone for two months, you could provide an accrual of two-thirds of the previous bill, making adjustments if that bill is considered to be unusually high or low. The decision as to how much to set aside as the accrual may in some cases be a rough estimate, but with thought it is unlikely to be too far wrong.

3 Prepayments

3.1 Prepayments, as the name suggests, is the payment in advance for certain expenses. For example, rates may be payable 12 months in advance in March for the year March to February next. If the accounting period ends 31 December, two months will have been paid in advance.

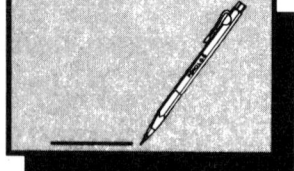

Student Activity 1

Using the same logic as when calculating accruals, how much is prepaid for rates if advance payment is made on 1 March for the six months March to August, and the accounting period ends on 30 April?

Feedback

3.2 In this case only four months should be reflected in the accounts as a prepaid expense covering the period from May to August.

4 How accruals and prepayments are dealt with in the accounts

4.1 To understand how accruals and prepayments are dealt with in the accounts you must remember what has actually happened. So, with accruals, the proportion relating to the current accounting period is owed by the firm so it is a liability a commitment that will have to be met at some stage. The amount of the accrual is therefore included in the profit and loss account with the other expenses and in the balance sheet under the current liabilities as an accrued expense, as shown below.

Current liabilities:
Creditors	XX
Accrued expenses	XX
Bank overdraft	XX
	XX

4.2 The prepayment, because it is a payment made in advance of the expense, is therefore an asset to the firm. So in the profit and loss account the amount apportioned to the current period is charged; using our earlier example of the rates this would be $^{10}/_{12}$ ths of the rates bill already paid where the accounting period ends on 31 December. The balance of the amount paid will appear in the balance sheet as Prepaid expenses in the current assets, as shown below.

Profit and loss account
Rent	XX
Wages	XX
Rates ($^{10}/_{12}$ ths)	XX
Accrued expenses:	
Telephone	XX
	XX

Current assets:
Stock	XX
Debtors	XX
Bank account	XX
Prepaid expenses ($^{2}/_{12}$ ths)	XX
	XX

4.3 Let us put some figures to this theoretical point:

During a year Choi pays the following rent:

Rent a/c Year 1

1 Jan	Bank	400
1 Apr	Bank	400
1 July	Bank	400

4.4 His annual rent is 1,600, so it is easy to see that that is what he needs to debit to his profit and loss account:

Profit and loss a/c

Rent	1,600	

Rent a/c Year 1

Transfer to profit and loss a/c	1,600	

4.5 Now put the two sides of the rent account together:

Rent a/c Year 1

1 Jan Bank	400	Transfer to profit		
1 Apr Bank	400	and loss a/c		1,600
1 July Bank	400			

4.6 You can see that Choi has only paid (in cash) 1,200, whereas he has debited his profit and loss with 1,600, which is his true rent. The rent account now has to be balanced off.

Rent a/c Year 1

1 Jan Bank	400	Dec 31	Transfer to		
1 Apr Bank	400		profit and loss a/c	1,600	
1 Jul Bank	400				
Balance c/d					
(to Year 2)	400				
	1,600			1,600	
		Year 2 Jan 1 balance b/d		400	
		(to balance sheet liability)			

4.7 We have brought down a balance of 400, which represents the amount unpaid (a credit = a liability).

4.8 So next year when Choi pays out his first money for rent, 400 will go to pay off the outstanding amount:

Rent a/c Year 2

21 Jan Bank	400	Yr 1	Balance b/d	400	

Bank a/c Year 2

1 Jan	Rent a/c	400

4.9 At this stage the rent account now stands at nil, as Choi has paid off last year's debt.

4.10 Obviously the reverse applies for a prepayment. Let us look at the above example but continue it on in Year 2.

Rent a/c Year 1

21 Jan	Bank	400	1 Jan	Balance b/d	400
1 Apr	Bank	800			
4 July	Bank	400			
10 Oct	Bank	400			
31 Dec	Bank	400			
		2,400			

4.11 Choi has paid out 2,400, less 400 he owed from last year = 2,000. He has overpaid by 400, and again he only needs 1,600 to be debited to his profit and loss account to represent a true year's profit. The additional 400 will be transferred to next year's books.

Rent a/c Year 2

21 Jan	Bank	400	1 Jan	Balance b/d	400
1 Apr	Bank	800	31 Dec	profit and loss A/c	1,600
4 July	Bank	400	31 Dec	Balance c/d	400
10 Oct	Bank	400		(to Year 3)	
31 Dec	Bank	400			
		2,400			2,400
Year 3					
1 Jan	Balance b/d	400			
	(to balance sheet)				

4.12 We have brought down a balance of 400 (a debit = an asset).

4.13 Finally, both carried-down balances will show on the balance sheet, because they have not been utilised during the year:

Extract from balance sheet Year 1

Current liabilities	
Accrued rent	400

Extract from balance sheet Year 2

Current assets	
Rent prepaid	400

4.14 A piece of advice: Accruals and prepayments usually form part of a question on trial balances. That is, the examiner gives you a trial balance and asks you to draw up a trading, profit and loss account and a balance sheet, bearing in mind certain items that have not yet been entered into the books. This will always include closing stock (opening stock being in the trial balance itself). In addition it will usually include some accruals and prepayments, as well as depreciation, which we will look at in the next Unit. Always take the trial balance figure as your starting point by transferring it to the profit and loss account and then underneath make the amendment (add accruals, deduct prepayments). Don't forget that those amending figures will also turn up in the balance sheet (they have not been double-entered; they are below the [trial balance] line).

4.15 So, the two figures above would be entered as follows:

Extract from trading and profit and loss account

Year 1	Rent	1,200		
	Add accrued	400		
			1,600	
Year 2	Rent	2,000		
	Less prepaid	400		
			1,600	

4.16 In both cases we arrived at the correct figure and the amendments will now show up in our balance sheet.

4.17 Try this straightforward example:

Student Activity 2

Trial balance of B. Black as at 31 December 19X1

	Dr £	Cr £
Capital		1,500
Purchases	10,000	
Sales		12,000
Opening stock	2,000	
Rent	1,000	
Rates	500	
	13,500	13,500

Notes:

- Closing stock is 3,000.
- Rent payable for the year is 1,500.
- Rates are prepaid by 100.

Required:

Draw up a trading profit and loss account and balance sheet for B. Black.

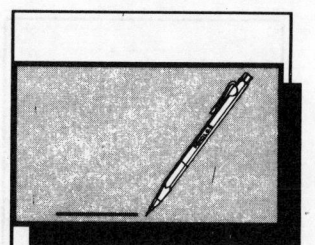

Feedback

4.18 Your trading profit and loss account and balance sheet should look like this:

B. Black
Trading profit and loss account for year ended 31 December 19X1

	£	£	£
Sales			12,000
Opening stock		2,000	
Add purchases		10,000	
		12,000	
Less closing stock		3,000	
Cost of goods sold			9,000
Gross profit			3,000
Less expenses:			
Rent	1,000		
Add accrued	500		
		1,500	
Rates	500		
Less prepaid	100		
		400	
			1,900
Net profit			1,100

B. Black
Balance sheet as at 31 December 19X1

Current assets		
Stock	3,000	
Prepaid rates	100	
	3,100	
Less current liabilities		
Rent accrued	500	
		2,600
Capital		1,500
Add net profit		1,100
		2,600

5 Bad debts

5.1 When goods are sold on credit there is an agreed period when payment is due from the debtor. If the debtor does not meet the commitment and the business judges it to be unlikely that the debt will be paid, then a provision is created to set aside these bad debts. It is prudent and realistic accounting to remove the expected benefit of payment from the accounts and present a more accurate picture. If at some stage the debtor does repay, then the bad debt can be written back and the benefit reflected in the accounts.

5.2 The amount of the provision for the bad debts should reflect the most likely assessment of non-payment and should not be too high or too low.

5.3 As this is money which is not expected to be received then it must be charged against the profit and loss account as bad debts written off. In the individual debtors T account the amount written off is credited and the bad debt account credited. So the debtors figure in the balance sheet will reflect the up-to-date position and no further adjustments have to be made.

A. Debtor a/c

1/1/XX	Stock	100	31/10/XX	Bad debts	100
		100			100

Bad debts a/c

31/10/XX	A. Debtor	100	Balance c/d	100
		100		100

Student Activity 3

Test your understanding of what we have covered so far. Write down in your own words the answers to the following questions.

(a) What is an accrual and why is it raised?

(b) What is a prepayment and how does it arise?

(c) How is an accrual dealt with in the accounts?

(d) How is a prepayment dealt with in the accounts?

(e) Why is a bad debt raised?

(f) How are the bad debts dealt with in the accounts?

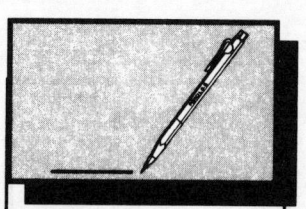

Feedback

5.4 Your answers should agree with these:

(a) An accrual is an account raised to show the benefit of some service/expense received but not paid for in the current accounting period. It is raised because there has been a benefit and this must be reflected in the accounts.

(b) A prepayment is a payment in advance and it arises because it is money that has been paid out but not all of it relates to the current accounting period.

(c) The amount of the accrual is debited to the profit and loss account and shown in the balance sheet under the current liabilities as an accrued expense.

(d) The amount of the prepayment related to the current accounting period is debited to the profit and loss account and it is entered on the balance sheet under current assets as prepaid expenses.

(e) Bad debts written off reflect the amounts that are not repaid by the debtors.

(f) The bad debts are charged against the profit and loss account. The debtors T account is credited and the bad debts account is debited.

6 Provision for bad debts

6.1 Bad debts are debtors we have identified during the year as being unlikely to repay us and so we have written off the debt against our profits.

6.2 However, during the same year there may be other debtors who we do not know about who will go bad later on. So if our debtors balance at the end of the year is 10,000 we can be pretty certain we will not actually receive all of it next year.

6.3 This presents us with a problem. The basic rule of accounting is that we must match current income against current expenditure (this is why we have accruals and prepayments). But how can we do this when we don't know exactly which debtor it is that will go bad? We have to do something, because this debt was incurred in this year's trading so we must find a way to put it against this years income.

6.4 The answer is that we cannot do anything that is 100 per cent accurate, but we can make an informed guess. Either we can scrutinise our accounts closely for tell-tale signs, and then make a provision for those which might go bad, or we can say something like past experience has taught me that 10 per cent of my debtors go bad in any one year, so I will make a provision out of this year's profits for debts which may go bad next year, but which were in fact incurred this year.

6.5   To do this we simply open an account called Provision for bad debts (sometimes called Provision for bad and doubtful debts) and transfer sufficient to cover our estimated losses next year out of our profits.

6.6   Debit profit and loss account, credit provision for bad debts account.

6.7   So in the example above our provision will be 1,000 (10% of 10,000).

Profit and loss a/c (extract) Year 1

Expenses	
Provision for bad debts account	1,000

Provision for bad debts a/c Year 1

	Profit and loss a/c	1,000

6.8   The outstanding balance then gets transferred to the balance sheet as it will be carried forward to the next year. Technically it is a liability, but for practical purposes it is deducted from the asset debtors to give a more accurate figure.

Extract from balance sheet Year 1

Current assets		
Debtors	10,000	
Less provision for bad debts	1,000	
		9,000

6.9   **Tip**: When working exercises, always treat bad debts account and Provision for bad debts account separately. Any bad debts next year will be transferred to a bad debts account and at the end of the year written off the profit and loss account. Any change in the amount of debtors will result in an adjustment to the provision for bad debts figure.

6.10 To continue our above example: in Year 2 debtors at the end total 15,000 so we require a bad debts provision of 10 per cent of 15,000 = 1,500. How much do we need to take out of the profit and loss account? Not 1,500, because we already have 1,000 towards it from last year; we need take only another 500.

Profit and loss a/c (extract) Year 2

Expenses increase in provision for bad debts	500

13

Provision for bad debts a/c

	Year 1 balance 1,000
	Year 2 profit and loss a/c 500
	1,500

Extract from balance sheet (Year 2)

Current assets	
Debtors 15,000	
Less provision for	
bad debts 1,500	
13,500	

6.11 The reverse will apply if the amount of debtors is less than last year:

Year 3 – Debtors 8,000. (Provision required 800.)

Profit and loss a/c (extract) Year 3

	Provision for bad debts a/c 700
	(i.e. 1,500 less 800; 700
	is re-credited to the profits)
	e.g. increase profit

Provision for bad debts a/c

Year 3 profit and loss a/c 700	Year 1 profit and loss A/c 1,000
Balance c/d 800	Year 2 profit and loss A/c 500
1,500	1,500
	Balance b/d 800

Extract from balance sheet Year 3

Debtors 8,000	
Less provision for bad debts 800	
7,200	

6.12 Now try this exercise

Student Activity 4

Trial balance of A. White as at 31 December 19X1

	Dr £	Cr £
Capital		15,000
Purchases	20,000	
Sales		24,000
Opening stock	4,000	
Rent	2,000	
Rates	1,500	
Debtors	12,000	
Bad debts	500	
Provision for bad debts		1,000
	40,000	40,000

Notes:

- Closing stock is 6,000

- Rent accrued is 1,000

- Rates are 1,000 per annum.

- Provision for bad debts is 10%.

Required:

Prepare A. Whites trading and profit and loss account and balance sheet.

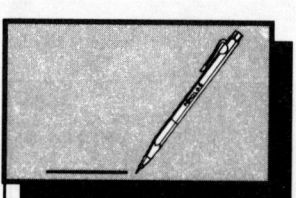

Feedback

6.13 Your trading and profit and loss account and balance sheet should look like these:

A. White
Trading profit and loss account for year ended 31 December 19X1

	£	£	£
Sales			24,000
Opening stock		4,000	
Add purchases		<u>20,000</u>	
		24,000	
Less closing stock		<u>6,000</u>	
Cost of goods sold			<u>18,000</u>
Gross profit			6,000
Less expenses:			
Rent	2,000		
Add accrued	<u>1,000</u>		
		3,000	
Rates	1,500		
Less prepaid	<u>500</u>		
		1,000	
Bad debts		500	
Increase in provision for bad debts		<u>200</u>	
			<u>4,700</u>
Net profit			<u>1,300</u>

A. White
Balance sheet as at 31 December 19X2

Current assets		
Stock		6,000
Debtors	12,000	
Less provision	<u>1,200</u>	
		10,800
Rates prepaid		<u>500</u>
		17,300
Less current liabilities		
Rent accrued		<u>1,000</u>
		<u>16,300</u>
Capital		
		15,000
Add net profit		<u>1,300</u>
		<u>16,300</u>

17

7 Summary

7.1 In this Unit you have begun to look at different ways in which the written up figures in a business books may need to be altered to stick to the accounting rule that current expenditure must be deducted from current income. The items you looked at were prepayments, accruals and provisions for bad debts.

7.2 You have seen how calculations are made to debtors less bad debts to arrive at figures for the provision for bad debts and at the balancing procedures for accruals and prepayments, as well as the way these are disclosed in the profit and loss account and balance sheet.

Self-assessment questions

1. What is a prepayment and where should it be shown on the balance sheet?

2. How is a prepayment dealt with in the profit and loss account?

3. What is an accrual and where should it be shown on the balance sheet?

4. How is an accrual dealt with in the profit and loss account.

5. What effects can the incorrect treatment of accruals and prepayments have on the net profit figure?

6. What is a bad debt, and what is the double entry treatment?

7. Why would a business have a provision for bad debts account?

8. Will an increase in the provision for bad debts increase or decrease the profit?

9. How are bad debts and provisions for bad debts disclosed in the profit and loss account and balance sheet?

10. Why are adjustments made in the accounts for accruals prepayments, bad debts and provisions for bad debts?

3 What fixed assets are depreciated?

3.1 Fixed assets such as equipment and vehicles are depreciated. Land is not usually depreciated as the land does not wear out unless it is a quarry, mine or suchlike. Freehold property is usually depreciated although some organisations, typically banks, claim that their buildings are kept in such good repair that they do not need to be depreciated.

4 Why are fixed assets depreciated?

4.1 It is inevitable that at some time these fixed assets (such as equipment and vehicles), will need to be replaced. So if a van is bought for 5,000 and its expected life is five years, you must look at the decreasing value of this asset and prepare for its replacement. By depreciating the asset over its expected life, yet setting a proportion of its value against the profit and loss account for this period, the cost of the fixed asset reduces the profit over the expected life by depreciating its value.

5 Main methods of depreciation

5.1 There are two main methods of depreciation that can be used:

- the straight-line method
- the reducing balance method.

The straight-line method

5.2 This is the most commonly used method. It is an equal division of the cost of the fixed asset, less any resale value, over the expected life. An example is:

Cost of fixed asset	£1,000
Resale/scrap value	£40
Expected life	two years

So: $\dfrac{£1,000 - £40}{\text{Expected life}} = \dfrac{960}{2 \text{ years}}$

= £480 depreciation per annum

5.3 This is a simple example to help you understand the principle. This method is called the straight-line method because if the annual amounts of depreciation were plotted on a graph and all the points joined, you would have a straight line.

The reducing balance method

5.4 This method is based on a fixed percentage being depreciated from the outstanding value of the fixed asset. So in Year 1 this would be the cost of the fixed asset. Then in subsequent years the fixed percentage is applied against the outstanding figure and so on. The resale or scrap value is not deducted from the value of the fixed asset.

Unit 5

Depreciation

> **Objectives**
>
> At the end of this Unit you will be able to:
> - define depreciation
> - explain why depreciation is used
> - calculate depreciation using the two main methods
> - deal with depreciation in the accounts
> - carry out the correct accounting procedures for the sale of a fixed asset.

1 Introduction

1.1 A set of accounts should give as accurate as picture a possible of a business's financial position at a particular time. As relevant transactions do not necessarily take place within an accounting period, adjustments such as accruals and prepayments, looked at in Unit 4, must be made.

1.2 A similar problem arises with fixed assets, such as plant and machinery. An item may be completely paid for within one accounting period, but it will be purchased with the intention of using it over several years. By the end of this time, it may be worthless and so need to be written out of the accounts. If only the purchase price and the writing-out value were included in the accounts a false picture of its value to the business in each year of its life would not be shown. An adjustment, called depreciation, is therefore made to reflect the value of the asset to the business during each year of its life.

2 What is depreciation?

2.1 Depreciation is the means of gradually reducing the value of a fixed asset in the accounts. The cost of a fixed asset is capital expenditure and as such it is not charged to the profit and loss account, but its value is adjusted in the balance sheet. As the asset may have an expected life of, say, five years, then depreciation is the accounting tool to reduce its value over this period to nil or its expected resale or scrap value.

5.5   The percentage is calculated by using the following formula:

$$1 - n\sqrt{\frac{s}{c}}$$

n = number of years   s = scrap value   c = cost

5.6   We'll use the same example to calculate the depreciation using this method:

Cost of fixed asset	1,000
Resale or scrap value	40
Expected life	two years
Percentage depreciation	80%

Year 1

	£
Cost of fixed asset	1,000
80% of 1,000 =	800
	200

Year 2

	£
Book value	200
80% of 200 =	160
Resale/scrap value	40

5.7   So at the end of Year 2 we are left with the resale or scrap value. Even by using this simple example you can see how the different methods charge very different amounts in the two years to arrive at the same answer:

- straight-line: depreciation at 480 for each of the two years.

- reducing balance: depreciation Year 1 800, Year 2 160.

5.8   The two methods reflect different assessments of the asset. The reducing balance is probably the most realistic as fixed assets depreciate at a much higher rate at the beginning of their life. You only have to look at a new car to see how quickly its value depreciates in the first 12 months. It can also be argued that towards the end of the asset's life the repair costs will be greater, and by using this method a smaller amount of depreciation is charged so there is a more equitable spread of the expenses. With the straight-line method charging the same amount each year, in later years with repair bills there would be a marked effect on the profit.

5.9   Whatever method is adopted by the business, it must be used throughout its existence. If the firm wants to change the method it must explain what effects this change will have on the profit and loss in the accounts. This is required under the rules set out for accounting practice.

Student Activity 1

Calculate the depreciation using both methods for the following:

Fixed asset cost	10,000
Resale or scrap value	1,250
Expected life	3 years
Percentage depreciation if required	50%

Feedback

5.10 Your calculations should agree with these:

Straight-line method:
$$\text{Cost } 10,000 - 1,250 = \frac{8,750}{3}$$
An annual charge of 2,916.66 for two years, final year charge of 2,916.68.

Reducing balance method

Year 1

	£
Cost of fixed assets	10,000
50% of 10,000	5,000
	5,000

Year 2

	£
Book value	5,000
50% of 5,000	2,500
	2,500

Year 3

	£
Book value	2,500
50% of 2,500	1,250
	1,250

6 How depreciation is dealt with in the accounts

6.1 As you know, depreciation (by whichever method is adopted) is based on the expected life of the fixed asset. It is this annual amount of depreciation that is charged against the profit and loss account and so it is included in the businesss expenses. It is, therefore, part of the expenses that reduce the gross profit.

6.2 In the balance sheet the value of the fixed asset must be reduced by the accumulated depreciation to show the new value of the fixed asset. It will be expressed as follows:

	£
Vehicles	5,000
Less provision for depreciation	1,000
New value	4,000

6.3 Here is an example of how depreciation is treated in the accounts.
Smith & Co. bought an asset for 22,000 in Year 1. It is to be depreciated by 25% on the straight-line method, and is expected to have a scrap value of 2,000. Therefore depreciation is 5,000 per annum (22,000 less 2,000 x 4).

Profit and loss a/c

Year 1	Provision for depreciation	5,000
Year 2	Provision for depreciation	5,000
Year 3	Provision for depreciation	5,000
Year 4	Provision for depreciation	5,000

Provision for depreciation a/c

Year 1	Profit and loss a/c	5,000
Year 2	Profit and loss a/c	5,000
Year 3	Profit and loss a/c	5,000
Year 4	Profit and loss a/c	5,000
		20,000

Extracts from balance sheets

	Cost	Dep.	NBV
Asset Year 1	22,000	5,000	17,000
Asset Year 2	22,000	10,000	12,000
Asset Year 3	22,000	15,000	7,000
Asset Year 4	22,000	20,000	2,000

6.4 This leaves 2,000, being the scrap value; we will see later what happens with this.

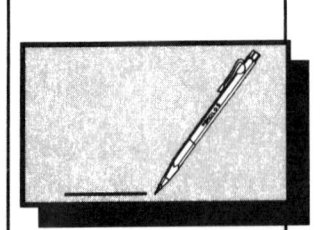

6.5 Now tackle the following activity on separate sheets of paper.

Student Activity 2

Draw up the trading profit and loss account and balance sheet from the following information, for D. Trader as at 31 December 19XX:

	£
Freehold premises	25,000
Vehicles (to be depreciated straight-line over 5 years)	6,000
Equipment (to be depreciated straight-line over 10 years)	15,000
Stock	5,000
Debtors	1,000
Creditors	3,000
Bank O/D	5,100
Sales	25,000
Purchases	10,000
Opening stock	6,500
Drawings	3,000
Rates	750
Salaries	6,000
Heating and lighting	350
Returns outwards	500
Capital	40,000

Feedback

6.6   Your trading and profit and loss account should look like this:

**D. Trader trading profit and loss account
for the year ended 31 December 19XX**

	£	£	£
Sales			25,000
Opening stock		6,500	
Add purchases	10,000		
Less returns out	500		
		9,500	
		16,000	
Less closing stock		5,000	
Cost of goods sold			11,000
Gross profit			14,000
Less expenses:			
Rates		750	
Salaries		6,000	
Heating and lighting		350	
Depreciation:			
Vehicles		1,200	
Equipment		1,500	
			9,800
Net profit			4,200

D. Trader
Balance sheet as at 31 December 19XX

Fixed assets

	Cost	Dep.	NBV
Premises	25,000	–	25,000
Equipment	15,000	1,500	13,500
Vehicles	6,000	1,200	4,800
	46,000	2,700	43,300

Current assets
Stock	5,000	
Debtors	1,000	
		6,000

Current liabilities
Creditors	3,000	
Bank O/D	5,100	
	8,100	
		(2,100)
		41,200
Capital		40,000
Net profit		4,200
		44,200
Drawings		3,000
		41,200

6.7 Now that you know how to work out the depreciation of fixed assets and how it is reflected in the accounts, we will look at the disposal or sale of one of these assets.

7 Why fixed assets are sold

7.1 From time to time some of the fixed assets will need to be replaced because of changes in technology or in order to update existing equipment. If they are not, it may cost the firm money in terms of repair bills, lost production time and maybe lost orders if they cannot produce the goods on time.

8 The accounting procedure for the disposal of a fixed asset

8.1 Over the expected life of the fixed asset, the annual depreciation charges have been set aside in an account called the Provision for depreciation account. This is a bookkeeping account that records each year's depreciation charges. There is also a similar account for the fixed assets, which shows the cost of the equipment or vehicles bought and the sale of these items.

8.2 It is important for you at this stage merely to understand the principle so that you can appreciate what happens when the fixed asset is sold.

8.3 If some equipment had been depreciated over the last five years at 1,000 per annum, with the original cost being 6,000, it is now time to change this equipment. At the outset there was an expected resale or scrap value of 1,000, and, if the sale of this equipment does provide 1,000, then the depreciation, resale value and expected life were exactly right. So in the accounts for this item the only action to take is to remove its value from the balance sheet, because everything else was right.

Student Activity 3

The above is an ideal situation, but unfortunately things don't always work out this well. What will happen if the sale price is less than or more than the depreciated value of the fixed asset?

Feedback

8.4 You should have identified that there will be a 'profit' or 'loss' on the transaction. But are these conventional losses and profits which affect the profit and loss account?

8.5 Let us look at what you do if the depreciation is short. This is best explained by example: if the equipment costing 6,000 were depreciated at 1,000 per annum but the resale proceeds were only 500 instead of 1,000 then it is short by 500. In the accounts, this piece of equipment is still removed from the balance sheet, but because only 5,000 has been provided for, an entry must be passed for 500.

	£
Cost of fixed asset	6,000
5 years depreciation @ 1,000	5,000
	1,000
Sale proceeds	500
Shortfall	500

8.6 This is dealt with by debiting the profit and loss account with 500, noted as depreciation under-provided for. This will balance the accounts. The same procedure will apply if the fixed asset is sold before the end of its expected life, and insufficient depreciation has been provided for to date.

8.7 The other side of the equation is if there is a profit on resale. Using the same example, let us consider:

	£
Cost	6,000
Depreciation: 5 years @ 1,000	5,000
	1,000
Sale proceeds	2,000
Profit	1,000

8.8 There is therefore a profit of 1,000 plus the expected resale value of 1,000. The 2,000 sale proceeds represent 1,000 profit, and this is calculated in a bookkeeping account called Disposal of fixed assets account, where the profit or loss is calculated.

Disposal of fixed assets account

	£		£
Fixed asset at cost	6,000	Proceeds	2,000
Profit and disposal	1,000	Depreciation	5,000
	7,000		7,000

8.9 The account must balance. In the accounts the 1,000 profit is applied to the credit side of the profit and loss account, as follows:

	£
Gross profit	5,000
Add profit on disposal of fixed asset	1,000
	6,000
Less expenses	3,000
Net profit	3,000

Student Activity 4

From the following, calculate the profit or loss on the sale of the fixed assets by using the disposal of fixed assets account. State what will happen in the accounts on each occasion. Write your answers on separate sheets of paper.

(a)   Cost 3,500

Straight-line depreciation for three years, 500 resale value. Sale proceeds 750 after three years.

(b)   Cost 5,000

Straight-line depreciation for four years, no resale value. Sold for 1,000 after three years.

(c)   Cost 10,000

Straight-line depreciation for five years, resale value 1,000, sold for 2,000 after four years.

(d)   Cost 7,500

Straight-line depreciation for four years, resale value 500, sold after four years for 750.

Feedback

8.10   Your calculations should agree with these:

(a)

Disposal of fixed assets account

	£		£
Fixed asset of cost	3,500	Proceeds	750
profit on disposal	250	Depreciation	3,000
	3,750		3,750

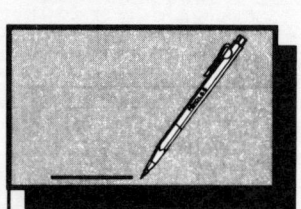

8.11   The fixed asset is removed from the balance sheet and the profit and loss account is credited with 250.

(b)

Disposal of fixed assets account

	£		£
Fixed asset at cost	5,000	Proceeds	1,000
		Depreciation	3,750
		Loss on disposal	250
	5,000		5,000

8.12 The fixed asset is removed from the balance sheet and the profit and loss account is charged/debited 250 with depreciation under-provided for.

(c)
Disposal of fixed assets account

	£		£
Fixed asset at cost	10,000	Proceeds	2,000
		Depreciation	7,200
		Loss on disposal	800
	10,000		10,000

8.13 The fixed asset is removed from the balance sheet, and the profit and loss account debited with 800 depreciation under-provided for.

(d)
Disposal of fixed assets account

	£		£
Fixed asset at cost	7,500	Proceeds	750
Profit on disposal	250	Depreciation	7,000
	7,750		7,750

8.14 The fixed asset is removed from the balance sheet, and the profit and loss account credited 250.

8.15 Although in the previous answers the sales with a loss were also sold before the end of their expected life, it could also be noted as loss of sale of fixed asset.

8.16 There is only one other point to consider and that is that some firms may charge depreciation monthly. This does not create any real problems if the accounts are still drawn up annually. If, however, a fixed asset is sold part way through the year, then the depreciation will be the accumulated months until the sale (e.g. sold three months into the year, so three months depreciation only is charged for the item sold). If a replacement is bought at the same time then it will have nine months depreciation charged.

9 Summary

9.1 In this Unit you have seen how to work out and deal with the annual depreciation charge, how to assess if a profit or loss has been made on the sale of a fixed asset and how it is dealt with in the accounts. You have had an opportunity to complete some exercises in working out the depreciation and the outcome on disposal, using the two main methods, which are the straight-line and reducing balance methods.

9.2 Note: You have now completed the main elements of accounting required by the course. At this stage you should take stock and make sure you fully understand the following:

- how to enter accounts into ledgers
- how to balance them off
- how to take out a trial balance from a set of books
- how to draw up a trading profit and loss account and balance sheet from a trial balance
- how to deal with accruals, prepayments and provisions for bad debts and provision for depreciation.

Self-assessment questions

1. Define depreciation.

2. What is the purpose of charging depreciation on fixed assets?

3. What are the two main methods of depreciation?

4. Give the formula for the most common method of depreciation.

5. Give the formula for the most appropriate form of depreciation for an asset that wears out rapidly at the beginning of its life.

6. What items are estimates in working out depreciation?

7. From the following calculate the depreciation charge for the next three years.

    Fixed asset cost   150,000

    Depreciates 30% per annum, reducing balance method.

8. Work out the profit of loss of the above item if it were sold after year three for 45,000.

9. How is depreciation disclosed in the profit and loss account?

10. How is depreciation shown in the balance sheet?

15

Unit 6

Partnership Accounts

> **Objectives**
>
> At the end of this Unit you will be able to:
> - define a partnership
> - identify the legislation relevant to partnerships
> - prepare and make entries in partnership accounts
> - prepare and make entries in partnership appropriation and current accounts
> - draw up a partnership balance sheet.

1 Introduction

1.1 You have looked at general bookkeeping techniques, which are applicable to all kinds of business. However, there are additional factors relevant for specific types of organisation.

1.2 In this Unit, we shall look at the matters specific to partnerships, why they exist, how they arise and how to apply them. You will see that the major differences between accounting for partnerships and other forms of business are associated with the sharing of profits and how each partner relates to the business.

2 What is a partnership?

2.1 The Partnership Act 1890 describes a partnership as the relationship which exists between persons carrying on a business in common with a view of profit. So there is more than one person, and they have a business to run to make a profit.

2.2 The maximum number of partners allowed is 20, although there are some exceptions, such as firms of chartered accountants.

2.3 There is usually a partnership agreement drawn up which states such things as:

- the capital to be contributed by each partner
- how the profits and losses are to be divided
- interest to be paid on partner's loans
- partners' drawings
- what is to happen if a partner leaves/retires from the firm and a new partner is to be bought in to retain the status quo.

2.4 If no formal agreement (the Partnership Agreement) is held, the Partnership Act 1890 states that the rules to be followed are:

- all profits and losses to be shared equally among the partners
- no interest on capital is payable, or for conducting the business
- partners are entitled to 5% interest on loans above the amount of capital
- every partner is allowed to take part in the management of the business
- all existing partners need to agree to the inclusion of a new partner.

2.5 These then are the rules which govern partnerships, decided either by the partners or by utilising the Partnership Act 1890. Now we will look at how the accounts are dealt with for partnerships.

3 The accounts of partnerships

3.1 The trading profit and loss account is calculated in the usual way to arrive at the net profit. It is at this point, however, that we have a change: the profits have to be divided between the partners in the agreed ratio. This calculation takes place in the appropriation account, an account which is presented after the net profit line. If there is a loss, this will be divided in exactly the same proportions.

The following is an example:

3.2 The net profit is 10,000 and profits are to be divided equally between the two partners.

Appropriation account

Net profit		10,000
Less profits shared 50 % partner 1	5,000	
Less profits shared 50 % partner 2	5,000	10,000

Student Activity 1

Using the same profit figure, 10,000, but divided on a ratio of 3:2, draw up the appropriation account.

Feedback

3.3   Your appropriation account should look like this:

Appropriation account

Net profits		10,000
Less profits shared 60% partner 1	6,000	
Less profits shared 40% partner 2	4,000	10,000

3.4   The heading for the appropriation account is in the same format as for the trading profit and loss account, e.g:

A and B Partnership
Appropriation account for the year ended 31 December 19XX

3.5   The appropriation account is not only used to assess the division of profits or losses but for the salaries, interest on loans and interest on capital. Only when all this has been divided are the figures carried to the balance sheet.

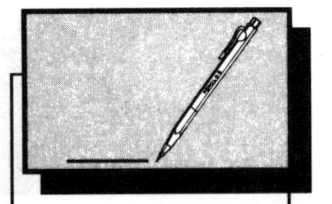

Student Activity 2

Draw up the appropriation account for X, Y and Z for the year ended 31 December 19XX, using the following information:

	£
Net Profit	15,000
Salary X	5,000
Salary Y	3,000
Salary Z	10,000
Interest on capital X	500
Interest on capital Y	500
Interest on capital Z	1,500

Profits/losses to be divided on 2:3:5 i.e. X:Y:Z.

Feedback

3.6 Your appropriation account should be in a similar form of presentation to that you have seen earlier.

X, Y and Z
Appropriation account for the year ended 31 December 19XX

		£	£
Net profit			15,000
Less	Salary X	5,000	
	Salary Y	3,000	
	Salary Z	10,000	
			18,000
Less	Interest X	500	
	Interest Y	500	
	Interest Z	1,500	
			2,500
Loss			(5,500)
	Shared X	(1,100)	
	Shared Y	(1,650)	
	Shared Z	(2,750)	
			(5,500)

3.7 The money put into the partnership is known as the capital account, and one capital account is held for each individual partner. This is the money put in to finance the business. For day-to-day transactions between the business and the partners' current accounts are held, i.e. drawings.

3.8 These accounts are presented in the balance sheet. The profits and losses are added to or deducted from the individual partner's current accounts, in the same way that interest received and payable and salaries are also passed to the current accounts. The capital accounts remain in the original investment level unless there is a need for additional capital, at which time the partners will put in the additional funds in the same proportions as the original sum.

3.9 The balance sheet would therefore look like this:

A and B
Balance sheet as at 30 June 19XX

Fixed assets			
Premises			10,000
Current assets			
Stock	3,000		
Debtors	1,500		
Bank	<u>1,127</u>		
		5,627	
Current liabilities			
Creditors		<u>500</u>	
			<u>5,127</u>
			<u>15,127</u>
Capital accounts			
A		5,000	
B		<u>5,000</u>	
			10,000
Current accounts			
A		2,500	
B		<u>2,627</u>	
			<u>5,127</u>
			<u>15,127</u>

3.10 Now try the following exercise to check your understanding. Complete your answer on separate sheets of paper.

Student Activity 3

Draw up the appropriation account and balance sheet for Jones & Smith for the year ended 30 June 19XX.

Net profit	15,000
Salary: Jones	3,000
Smith	2,000

balance divided equally

Capital accounts:
Jones	10,000
Smith	10,000

Current accounts as at 29 June 19XX:
Jones	2,150
Smith	1,900
Creditors	1,575
Debtors	1,650
Stock	3,500
Premises	30,000
Bank	4,975
Cash	500

Feedback

3.11 Your appropriation account and balance sheet should look like these:

Jones & Smith
Appropriation account for the year ended 30 June 19XX

			£	£
Net profit				15,000
Less salary	Jones		3,000	
	Smith		2,000	5,000
				10,000
Shared	50% Jones		5,000	
	50% Smith		5,000	10,000

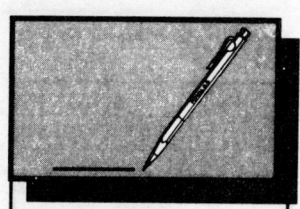

Jones & Smith
Balance sheet as at 30 June 19XX

	£	£	£
Fixed assets			
Premises			30,000
Current assets			
Stock	3,500		
Debtors	1,650		
Bank	4,975		
Cash	500		
		10,625	
Less current liabilities			
Creditors		1,575	
			9,050
			39,050
Capital: Jones		10,000	
Smith		10,000	
			20,000
Current: Jones		10,150	
Smith		8,900	
			19,050
			39,050

4 Working the accounts

4.1 For examination purposes it is recommended that you show how you arrived at the partners' new balance. The reason for this is that if you have made any errors, the examiner can give you credit for what you have done right, whereas if your final figure is wrong you will lose all marks for that part of the question.

4.2 So, going back to Activity 3, there are two ways you can do this: either by showing the partners' current accounts, example (1), or by incorporating the sum into the balance sheet, example (2).

Example (1)
Jones current a/c

Balance c/d	10,150	Balance b/d (from trial balance)	2,150
		Salary	3,000
		Share of profits	5,000
	10,150		10,150
		Balance b/d (to balance sheet)	10,150

	Smiths current a/c	
Balance c/d 8,900	Balance b/d	1,900
	(from trial balance)	
	Salary	2,000
	Share of profits	5,000
8,900		8,900
	Balance b/d	
	(to balance sheet)	8,900

Example (2)
Balance sheet

	£	£	£
Fixed assets			
Premises			30,000
Current assets			
Stock	3,500		
Debtors	1,650		
Bank	4,975		
Cash	500		
	10,625		
Current liabilities			
Creditors		1,575	
			9,050
			39,050
Capital account			
Jones		10,000	
Smith		10,000	
			20,000
Current accounts	**Jones**	**Smith**	
Balance b/f	2,150	1,900	
Add Salary	3,000	2,000	
Add profits	5,000	5,000	
	10,150	8,900	19,050
			39,050

5 Interest and drawings

5.1 Two other points to note about partnership accounts are :

5.2 Partners sometimes pay each other interest on their capital accounts. This is because if one partner has put much more capital into a partnership than another, he or she deserves some additional remuneration, especially if the division of profits is not in the same ratio as the capital. This interest must be agreed by the partnership.

5.3 Drawings will be deducted from the partners' current accounts. Usually each partner will have an agreed amount they can take out of the business, usually as a withdrawal of salary or profits. Sometimes partners agree to pay interest on these drawings. The reason is as follows: suppose Smith & Jones are in partnership. Each one makes drawings of 10,000, Smith on January 1, Jones on December 31. Smith obviously benefits from this, as he could, for example, put it in a deposit account and earn interest on it, whereas Jones' money is staying in the business for the whole year and helping both of them to earn profits. Interest on drawings is charged to each partners current account and credited back to the appropriation account before the profits are shared, usually on a percentage per annum basis. An example is given below:

Smith & Jones have a capital sum of 10,000 each. Smith's current account balance is 2,342 and Jones' current account balance is 3,600.

Net profits of 15,000 are shared equally after taking the following into consideration.

(1)	Salaries	Jones	£1,525	
		Smith	2,000	
(2)	Interest on capital		5%	
(3)	Interest on drawings		10% per annum	
(4)	Drawings	Smith	3,000	(1 April)
		Jones	2,000	(1 July)

Working

Profit and loss appropriation a/c

		£	£
Net profit b/d			15,000
Add interest on drawings	Smith	225	
	Jones	100	
			325
			15,325
Less salaries	Smith	2,000	
	Jones	1,525	
			(3,525)
Less interest on capital	Smith	500	
	Jones	500	
			(1,000)
			10,800
profits shared	50% Smith	5,400	
	50% Jones	5,400	
			10,800

Current a/c Smith

	£		£
Interest on drawings	225	Balance b/d	2,342
Drawings	3,000	Salary 2,000	
Balance c/d	7,017	Interest on capital	500
		Share of profits	5,400
	10,242		10,242

Current a/c Jones

	£		£
Interest on drawings	100	Balance b/d	3,600
Drawings	2,000	Salary	1,525
Balance c/d	8,925	Interest on capital	500
		Share of profits	5,400
	11,025		11,025

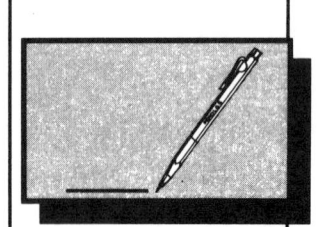

5.4 Use the following exercise to develop workings fully. Draw up your answer on separate sheets of paper.

Student Activity 4

Robin, John and Alison are in business as partners. Each has put 15,000 into the partnership on 1 January 19X1. The following information is relevant as at 31 December 19X1:

- Drawings:

    Robin – 3,000 on 1 July

    John – 4,000 on 1 April

    Alison – 3,600 on 1 October

- Net profit – 25,020

- Current account balances:

    Robin – 2,000 cr

    John – 3,000 cr

    Alison – 3,000 cr

- Interest on drawings – 5% per annum

- Interest on capital – 10% per annum

Required:

Prepare an appropriation account and current accounts for all three partners.

Feedback

5.5 Your profit and loss appropriation account and current accounts should agree with these:

Profit and loss appropriation account

Net profit b/d			25,020
Add interest on drawings			
	Robin	75	
	John	150	
	Alison	<u>45</u>	
			<u>270</u>
			25,290
Less interest on capital:			
	Robin	1,500	
	John	1,500	
	Alison	<u>1,500</u>	
			<u>(4,500)</u>
Profits shared equally:			<u>20,790</u>
	Robin	6,930	
	John	6,930	
	Alison	<u>6,930</u>	
			<u>20,790</u>

Current a/c Robin

	£		£
Interest on drawings	75	Balance b/d	2,000
Drawings	3,000	Interest on capital	1,500
Balance c/d	<u>7,355</u>	Share of profits	<u>6,930</u>
	10,430		10,430
		Balance b/d	7,355*

Current a/c John

	£		£
Interest on drawings	150	Balance b/d	3,000
Drawings	4,000	Interest on capital	1,500
Balance c/d	<u>7,280</u>	Share of profits	<u>6,930</u>
	11,430		11,430
		Balance b/d	7,280*

Current a/c Alison

	£		£
Interest on drawings	45	Balance b/d	3,000
Drawings	3,600	Interest on capital	1,500
Balance c/d	7,785	Share of profits	6,930
	11,430		11,430
		Balance b/d	7,785*

*If you show these accounts in an examination you may transfer only the balance b/d to the final balance sheet, otherwise you must show all workings in the balance sheet as explained above

Admission or retirement of a partner

5.6 Sometimes a business will take on another partner, or a partner may retire. Most businesss will take advantage of this situation by incorporating goodwill into the original/remaining partners' accounts. goodwill is the amount paid in excess of the value of the assets.

5.7 goodwill can arise because of:

- the trade and custom you inherit
- the skilled/trained staff you inherit
- location of the business
- good connections with suppliers
- trade marks, patents etc.
- monopoly position.

5.8 We'll look at the inclusion of goodwill into the books of a partnership.

5.9 Apple & Pear are in partnership sharing profits and losses equally. They decide to take on Apricot and change the partnership agreement to:

Apple   40%
Pear   40%
Apricot   20%

5.10 On inclusion of Apricot they decide to bring goodwill to the value of 20,000.

5.11 The double entry requirements for this transaction will be:

Debit	Goodwill account	20,000
Credit	Apple (capital a/c)	10,000 (50%) old profit
Credit	Pear (capital a/c)	10,000 (50%) sharing ratio

5.12 This amount will increase Apple's and Pear's capital accounts.

5.13 If the partnership decides to write off the goodwill immediately, the double entry will be:

Debit	Apple (capital a/c)	8,000 (40%) new profit
Debit	Pear (capital a/c)	8,000 (40%) sharing
Debit	Apricot (capital a/c)	4,000 (20%) ratio
Credit	goodwill	20,000

5.14 This will have the effect of decreasing the partners' capital accounts. Note that Apricot is debited when the goodwill is written off but is not included when the goodwill is introduced. This will always be the case.

Remember:

Debit goodwill on introduction
Credit capital accounts in old ratios of goodwill

Debit capital accounts in new ratios on elimination
Credit goodwill on elimination.

5.15 Sometimes, assets will be revalued on admission of a partner. The accounting treatment is as follows:

5.16 Usually assets will increase, therefore:

Debit the asset with the increase
Credit the partners' capital accounts in their profit sharing ratio with the increase.

5.17 Using the same partners as before, if we decide to revalue the premises from 120,000 to 150,000 the entries will be:

Debit	Premises	30,000
Credit	Apple	15,000
Credit	Pear	15,000.

5.18 Note that, like goodwill, the revaluation increases the old partners only in their old profit sharing ratios.

5.19 If a partner is taken on halfway through the accounting year and the profit ratios change you should split your appropriation account into two sections. An example is:

profit for the year 56,000
Apple and Pear share profits equally
Apricot joins in July (halfway through the accounting year)
The profits are shared, 40%, 40% and 20%).

5.20 The appropriation account will be as follows:

		Jan – June		July – Dec
Profit:		28,000		28,000
Less profit shared				
Apple	50%	14,000	40%	11,200
Pear	50%	14,000	40%	11,200
Apricot		–	20%	5,600
		28,000		28,000

5.21 If there are salaries and interest these should also be apportioned.

6 Summary

6.1 You have seen that partnerships are organisations set up by two or more people with an aim to make a profit. They are governed by partnership law and you have seen how to deal with the appropriation of profits in accordance with the partnership agreement or legal ruling. In addition, you should be able to show how these matters are dealt with in partners' current accounts and the balance sheet.

6.2 These illustrate how profits and losses are shared out between partners and the other transactions which take place for partners.

Self-assessment questions

1. What is a partnership?

2. What matters are contained in a partnership agreement?

3. State the rules contained within the Partnership Act of 1890 which are to be followed if no partnership agreement is held.

4. Why do partners charge interest on drawings and receive interest on capital?

5. Why do partners have current accounts and capital accounts?

6. Why do drawings appear in the current accounts of partners and not in the partnership appropriation account?

7. For what reasons does goodwill arise on the admission or retirement of a partner?

8. What is the accounting treatment of goodwill?

9. Draw up the appropriation account for C and D from the following information for the year ended 30 June 19XX.

    Net profit   £18,000

    Salary C   3,000

    Salary D   2,000

    Interest C   500

    Balance to be divided equally

10. Draw up the accounts for Doe and Dee for the year ended 31 June 19XX.

	£
Premises	15,000
Sales	20,000
Purchases	8,500
Salaries (workforce)	2,500
Rent and rates	1,500
Opening stock	4,000
Closing stock	3,500
Debtors	1,300
Creditors	2,600
Bank O/D	3,350

	Capital accounts	Current accounts
Doe	3,000	500
Dee	3,000	350

Partners both take a salary of 1,000. profits are divided equally.

Unit 7

Company Accounts

> **Objectives**
>
> At the end of this Unit you will be able to:
> - define a company
> - identify the legislation relevant for companies
> - draw up accounts for companies.

1 Introduction

1.1 Companies are brought into operation through the law, and legislation governs all that a company is entitled to do. It also specifies what information has to be included in accounts and how some items must be accounted for.

1.2 In this Unit, we will look at the impact of the law on company accounts and the implications this has on the ledger and final accounts.

2 What is a company?

2.1 A company is a separate legal entity. It must have at least two shareholders and capital is raised by selling shares. The company must be registered at Companies House. The law governing companies is the Companies Act 1985 and 1989.

2.2 There are several different types of company. They can be unlimited or limited; limited companies can be either private or public, which in turn relates to whether their shares are quoted or not on the Stock Exchange. The most common kind of company is the limited company; that is, the liability of its members (shareholders) is limited to the amount of their holding. Private limited companies tend to be small. The large companies, such as the banks we work for, are public limited companies, abbreviated to PLC. If a company is a public limited company then the PLC must always appear at the end of its name.

2.3 There are specific rules under the Companies Act 1985/89 as to how the accounts are to be presented, and we will in general be following these; a detailed knowledge is not required for this examination.

3 The accounts of limited companies

3.1 Although there are some differences, there are also many similarities between the limited company's account layout and that of the sole trader and partnership. The trading profit and loss account starts with turnover, which is the sales less the cost of the sales, i.e. cost of goods sold. It is calculated in the same way but not stated, to give the gross profit. The net profit is calculated as before but with less specific detail, as in reality there would be a great deal of information here which it is not necessary to publish. The figures are split in this example into distribution and administration expenses.

3.2 Next comes the appropriation account, which is included in the heading, for the distribution of the net profit. The items which are dealt with here are corporation tax, dividends and reserves. We will now look at each of these and at the provisions which appear above the line.

Corporation tax

3.3 Like individuals who pay income tax, companies pay corporation tax. The level of taxation is fixed in the governments budget, so it may change from year to year. It is payable on the taxable profits, not on the net profit, because the government allows various exemptions and allowances which will affect the amount payable. When the tax is payable depends on when the company was formed. So the amount you see in the accounts could relate to the last 12 months' profits or to an earlier period. A detailed knowledge of taxation is not required for your examination.

Dividends

3.4 The dividends represent the amount of the profit given back to the shareholders; they do not alter, directly, the value of their holding. It's a bit like the partnership which shared its profits, the difference here being that the directors decide what the dividend is to be and it can be different each year. If the company needs these funds, then a dividend may not be paid. Shareholders are looking for an investment with potential growth and one which will earn them an income: the dividend. Good dividends can in turn increase the stock value and vice versa, and if they are sold when the price has risen, the shareholder benefits.

Provisions

3.5 This is the amount which provides for depreciation, renewals or bad debts. It therefore encourages prudent accounting, in that unrealistic balances, i.e. for debtors, are not carried forward each period when a proportion of them is unlikely to be repaid.

Reserves

3.6 A reserve is a transfer from the profits to a reserve account designated by the directors. You may have heard of different types of reserve account, e.g. capital reserve, revenue reserve. This division has been seen to be simply the most realistic way to allocate the reserves so that they are available for specific uses.

3.7 The reserves are a means by which the company can provide for future expenditure that may have been planned but not yet implemented. They may be used to expand the business, or to ensure that there are sufficient funds to pay a dividend in the future, say, in the following year which at the moment the directors may feel is unlikely to be reached. It is like you or I putting away some money as savings so that it will be there in the case of an emergency.

3.8 There is one reserve, however, which is not created by transfers from the profits and this is the revaluation reserve. The major assets on the balance sheet such as the fixed assets, and in some cases the stock, are quoted at their historical cost, which can lead to a very unrealistic figure being quoted, say, for land and buildings. So from time to time these assets can be revalued. This is particularly important if the land or buildings were bought, say, 10 or 20 years ago. So the value of the asset after revaluation is the new valuation. The difference between the old historical cost and the new revalued figure is credited to the revaluation reserve account. The date of the revaluation will be reported in the notes to the accounts and they will include the basis of the valuation.

3.9 The reserves figure is added to the share capital in the balance sheet. The capital of a limited company is made up of shares which are sold to the public depending on the type of the company, as we have already discussed. There are different types of shares, the most common being ordinary and preference shares. The preference shares, as the name implies, get preference, and this preference is over the ordinary shareholder for the payment of dividends and the repayment of capital on liquidation.

3.10 The company has an authorised share capital and the face value of the share is known as its nominal value, e.g. 25p ordinary share. It is quite common for a company to have some shares which have not been issued, i.e. sold to the public, so that the authorised and the issued share capital may not be the same amount. The issued share capital, however, can never be greater than the authorised share capital.

3.11 If there are shares to be issued above the nominal or par value, then because all share issues must be recorded in the share capital account at their nominal value, the excess, i.e. the offer price over the nominal value, is transferred to the share premium account.

3.12 The capital and reserves are part of the balance sheet and will therefore be presented as follows:

Share capital   £

Authorised 100,000 ordinary shares at 1 each   100,000
Issued 50,000 ordinary shares at 1 fully paid   50,000
Share premium account   10,000
Revaluation reserve   50,000
General reserve   10,000
Retained profit   20,000

                                                  140,000

Student Activity 1

Draw up the capital part of the balance sheet from the following information:

Authorised capital, 500,000 1 ordinary shares. Issued 200,000 fully paid. There is no share premium account to date as the shares have been sold at par. A further 200,000 shares are to be issued at a price of 2 per share full paid.

Feedback

3.13 Your capital information should look like this:

Share capital	£
Authorised 500,000 ordinary shares at 1 each	500,000
Issued 400,000 ordinary shares at 1 fully paid	400,000
Share premium account	200,000
	600,000

3.14 Well now turn to the appropriation account, which is also an important feature of company accounting.

Student Activity 2

Draw up the appropriation account for X Y Z Ltd as at 31 December 19XX from the following information:

Net profit before tax 250,000

Tax 80,000

Dividend of 5p per share proposed. An interim dividend of 2p per share has been paid.

Total issued share capital 200,000 25p ordinary shares.

Retained profit at the beginning of the year 50,000.

Feedback

3.15 Your appropriation account should look like this:

XYZ Ltd
Appropriation account as at 31 December 19XX

		£	£
Net profit before tax			250,000
Less corporation tax			80,000
Net profit after tax			170,000
Less dividends:	paid	4,000	
	proposed	10,000	
			14,000
			156,000
Add retained profit 1 January 19XX			50,000
Retained profit 31 December 19XX			206,000

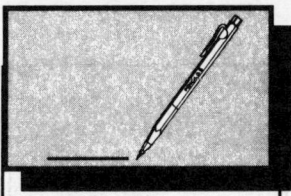

3.16 The retained profit figure of 206,000 will be transferred to the balance sheet.

3.17 We have now covered the major differences between company accounts and other types of account. Drawing up the accounts and finding the gross and net profit and balancing the balance sheet is the same process that we have already covered for sole traders and partnerships.

3.18 Note proposed dividends and taxation are unpaid at balance sheet date, so they have to be included in current liabilities section of the balance sheet.

3.19 Sometimes you may be asked by an examiner to say what reserves are and how they arise. Below are explanations of the major ones.

Share premium reserve

3.20 This arises when a company believes shareholders will pay more for the share than its nominal (face) value; usually companies issue shares at 1 each. This is rarely the same as the value of the company's shares on the Stock Exchange, which represents what the market considers a true reflection of the value of the whole company. So if a share of 1 nominal value is quoted on the Stock Exchange for 2, the company concerned would be silly to issue shares for just 1 each; shareholders would simply buy them up and sell them for a quick profit. Usually the company sets a price slightly below the market price to make sure the shareholders take up the new shares, but high enough to bring in some additional money for the company. An example is:

Smith & Co. Ltd have an issued share capital (being 10,000 shares at 1 each) of 10,000. They decide to sell a further 10,000 of shares for 1.50 a share.

Here is the original entry for the initial capital.

Capital a/c (ord 1 shares) (CR)

	Bank a/c	10,000

Bank a/c (DR)

Capital	10,000	

Now, when the company issues the additional shares, it can only credit the *nominal* value to the capital account, but receives 15,000 into the bank.

Capital a/c (ord 1 shares)

(old)	Bank	10,000
(new)	Bank	10,000

Bank a/c

(old)	Capital a/c	10,000	
(new)	Capital a/c	15,000	

The two entries do not balance, so in order to balance the entries we need to credit the extra 5,000 to a separate account. This is the account we call the share premium account.

Now the entries will read:

Capital a/c (1 ordinary shares)

(old)	Bank	10,000
(new)	Bank	10,000

Bank a/c

(old)	Capital a/c	10,000	
(new)	Capital a/c	10,000	
(new)	Share premium a/c	5,000	

Share premium a/c

(new)	Bank A/c	5,000

Revaluation reserve

3.21 Fixed assets such as motor vehicles are depreciated because they lose value. Premises, however, are usually the opposite, they tend to appreciate in value. It is unusual to take this into account every year, but there comes a time when the company has to say our premises are worth much more than the book value (i.e. the value in the accounts) so we must now reflect that in our books.

3.22 In order to do this the value of the asset must be raised, but something must be done to complete the double entry. This something is to increase the value of the reserves by establishing a revaluation reserve. An example is:

Jones & Co. Ltd have premises valued at 100,000, bought in 1985. They wish to reflect the current value, in their books, which has been stated to be 200,000 by a chartered surveyor.

Premises a/c

(old)	Bank a/c	100,000			
(new)	Revaluation a/c	100,000			

Bank a/c

			(old)	Premises	100,000

Revaluation reserve a/c

			(new)	Premises a/c	100,000

3.23 You will see from this that no actual cash goes out, it is simply a book entry to balance the increased value of the premises; it is a liability because it represents an increase in the value of the company to the shareholders.

General reserve

3.24 These are funds transferred from the retained profits account (i.e. the balance of the appropriation account) as an indication that they will not be available for distribution as dividends to the shareholders. It is not illegal to bring these back into the retained profits account and distribute them, but it is bad accounting practice, since it indicates that the company is not paying dividends out of present profits but past profits (i.e. it may well have made a loss this year, but by bringing funds down from the general reserve, it will keep its shareholders happy by paying a dividend).

Debentures

3.25 These are loans received by the company, which are usually for long periods, i.e. 10 years or more. They carry a fixed rate of interest which is paid as an expense in the profit and loss account. They appear as a long-term liability on the balance sheet.

Student Activity 3

Compare the ways in which interest on loans and dividends on shares are disclosed in company accounts.

Feedback

3.26 Interest is paid to outsiders who do not have any influence on the policies of companies and it is a charge on profits included in the profit and loss account. Dividends are paid to shareholders who are the owners of the company. These are, therefore, a way of sharing the profits among the owners and are appropriations of profit.

3.27 Any outstanding interest and dividends due but not paid by the company appear in the balance sheet as current liabilities.

Directors remuneration and auditors fees

3.28 These are both expenses and should be shown as an expense in the profit and loss account.

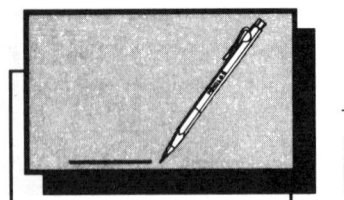

Student Activity 4

From the following information draw up a trading, profit and loss account for Gingers plc for the year ending 31 December 19X5. Draft your answer on separate sheets of paper.

Trial balance

	£000 Dr	£000 Cr
Sales		270
Purchases	87	
Stock 1.1.X5	36	
Fixed assets	345	
Debtors	40	
Creditors		30
Wages	16	
Rent	5	
Rates	3	
Motor expenses	1	
Administration expenses	2	
Directors' remuneration	30	
Debenture interest	1	
10% debenture		10
Ordinary shares		300
Dividend paid	3	
Bank	46	
Cash	5	
Retained profit 1 January 19X5		10
	620	620

Notes:

- Closing stock at 31 December 19X5 is £22,000.

- Final dividend proposed of 10%.

- Corporation tax payable 20,000.

- Transfer 30,000 to a general reserve.

Feedback

Gingers plc
Trading profit and loss account for year ended 31 December 19X5

	£000	£000
Sales		270
Opening stock	36	
Purchases	<u>87</u>	
	123	
Closing stock	<u>22</u>	
		<u>101</u>
Gross profit		169
Less expenses		
Wages	16	
Rent	5	
Rates	3	
Motor expenses	1	
Administration expenses	2	
Directors' remuneration	30	
Debenture interest	1	
		<u>58</u>
Net profit before tax		<u>111</u>

Appropriation account

Net profit b/d		111
Less corporation tax		<u>20</u>
Net profit after tax		91
Less:		
Dividends paid	3	
Dividends proposed	<u>30</u>	
		<u>33</u>
		58
Transfer to general reserve		<u>30</u>
		28
Add retained profit 1 January 19X5		<u>10</u>
Retained profit 31 December 19X5		<u>38</u>

Gingers plc
Balance sheet as at 31 December 19X5

	£000	£000	£000
Fixed assets			345
Current assets			
Stock	22		
Debtors	40		
Bank	46		
Cash	<u>5</u>		
		113	
Current liabilities			
Creditors	30		
Proposed dividends	30		
Corporation tax	<u>20</u>		
		80	
Working capital			<u>33</u>
Net assets			378
Less: Long-term liabilities			
10% debentures			<u>10</u>
			368
Capital + reserves			
Ordinary share capital			300
General reserve			30
Retained profits 31 December 19X5			<u>38</u>
			<u>368</u>

3.29 **Note**: The total of capital plus reserves is sometimes known as equity.

Types of Shares

3.30 Ordinary shares. These are the most common type of shares. They entitle the holder to a dividend out of the profits of the company. The rate of dividend is proposed by the directors and may vary from year to year. The directors take into account the profit and losses of the company, its cash and tax position before proposing a dividend. Normally the ordinary shareholder will have voting rights. The ordinary shareholder is the last person to be repaid out of the assets of the company should it go into liquidation.

3.31 Preference shares. A non-cumulative preference share is one that entitles the holder to a fixed rate of dividend (e.g. 10% preference shares). The rate of dividend is decided upon when the shares are authorised in the Memorandum of Association. Therefore, if the profits of the company increase, the preference shareholder will not benefit from an increase in dividend. However, as the name implies, these shares have preference over ordinary shares both in dividends and normally in repayment in liquidation. They are, therefore, a safer form of investment.

3.32 A cumulative preference share is better in that if a business is unable to pay its dividends in one year they are carried forward as arrears, and are payable in the next year. These are paid before ordinary shareholders.

Bonus issue

3.33 A bonus issue of shares is when a company issues free shares to existing shareholders without any money being paid for them. This is usually done to decrease revenue reserve, e.g. the profit and loss reserve, share premium reserve.

Rights issue

3.34 A rights issue is when shares are offered to existing shareholders at a lower price than the ruling market price. This has the advantage that the company will not be involved in issuing a prospectus to advertise the shares. Rights issues are usually underwritten by large investment and insurance companies.

4 Summary

4:1 In this Unit you have seen that the capital section of the balance sheet and the appropriation account which particularly distinguishes companies from partnerships and sole trader businesses.

4.2 Companies come into being and are run according to the provisions of the Companies Acts, and are owned by shareholders who are rewarded for their capital investment through dividends.

4.3 Shares are issued either at par or at a premium and the premiums per share are taken into a share premium Account. Shares can be issued as a rights issue which brings in cash, or as bonus issues which readjust the reserves. Companies may issue ordinary and preference shares of various types depending on requirements.

4.4 Company accounts contain various reserves:

- profit and loss account or retained profits built up from the retention of profits in the company

- general reserves similar to accumulated profits

- share premium account built up from the premiums on shares issued

- revaluation reserve reflecting the increase in value of land, property and so on.

4.5 Companies are able to issue a specific form of loan stock known as a debenture which may or may not be secured.

5 Self-assessment questions

1. Define a company.
2. What is limited liability?
3. What is a dividend?
4. What are reserves and how are they created?
5. Explain what is meant by a debenture?
6. What is equity?
7. Explain the difference between bonus and rights issues.
8. What are the differences between ordinary and preference shares?
9. What form of tax is paid by companies?
10. Explain the difference between a provision and a reserve.

Unit 8

Incomplete Records

> **Objectives**
>
> **At the end of this unit you will be able to:**
> - **define incomplete records**
> - **draw up a trading profit and loss account and balance sheet from incomplete records.**

1 Introduction

1.1 By now you should be quite familiar with the idea of drawing up a trading, profit and loss account and balance sheet for a sole trader, partnership or company from a trial balance and information about adjustments such as depreciation, bad debts, accruals and prepayments. However, what happens if you do not have a trial balance as your starting point? That's what we'll be looking at in this Unit.

1.2 Incomplete records can be a bit tricky to understand, so make sure you master one aspect before moving on to the next. The double entry principles underlying bookkeeping apply just as much here as in previous Units.

2 What are incomplete records?

2.1 Incomplete records are deemed to exist where only part of the transaction is recorded. Where a record of each transaction exists but it is not in a double entry bookkeeping system, it is known as single entry. We will concentrate on the former.

3 Why do incomplete records occur?

3.1 For very small concerns the keeping of a full set of books is onerous and to a large extent unnecessary. The cash book, creditors and debtors may well be sufficient for these purposes. It is therefore necessary from this limited, incomplete set of records to set about the formation of the accounts.

4 How to draw up the accounts from incomplete records

4.1 A good point to start from is the capital. Excluding any injection of capital the only way this figure is increased or decreased is by the net profit or loss. So, if at the end of Year 1 the capital were 5,000 and by the end of Year 2 it were 6,000, the net profit must have been 1,000. If there were drawings of 500 the profit must have been 1,500. We'll build on this by looking at an example.

	19X1 £	19X2 £
Equipment	500	400
Stock	250	300
Debtors	125	175
Bank	300	350
Creditors	300	125

4.2 This is all the information available, so we'll begin to draw up the accounts by starting with the balance sheet. This will help you to see how incomplete records work.

Balance sheet as at 31 December 19X1

	£	£	£
Fixed assets			
Equipment		500	
Current assets			
Stock	250		
Debtors	125		
Bank	300		
		675	
Less current liabilities			
Creditors		300	
Working capital			375
			875
Capital			?

Remember the equation:

Capital = Assets Liabilities - Liabilities

4.3 Therefore the capital figure must be 875

4.4 Moving on to Year 2, we can see how these accounts can be drawn up:

Balance sheet as at 31 December 19X2

	£	£	£
Fixed assets			
Equipment			400
Current assets			
Stock		300	
Debtors		175	
Bank		350	
		825	
Less current liabilities			
Creditors		125	
Working capital			700
			1,100
Capital 1 January 19X2			875
Net profit			?
Capital 31 December 19X2			1,100

4.5 Remembering the equation **C = A - L** we can insert the closing capital figure of 1,100, therefore the difference between closing capital + opening capital must be net profit

Student Activity 1

Calculate the net profit for the balance sheet above.

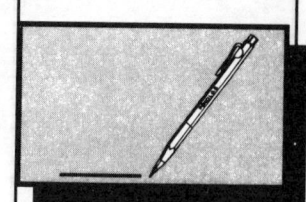

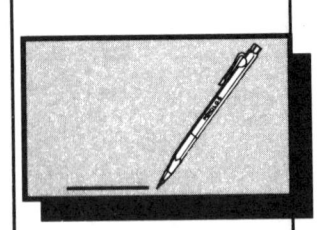

Feedback

4.6 You will see that the net profit for the year is the difference in capital between the two years:

31 December 19X2	1,100	Closing capital
1 January 19X2	875	Opening capital
	225	= Net profit for year

Student Activity 2

From the information given, draw up the balance sheets as at 31 December 19X1 and 19X2.

	19X1	19X2
Premises	12,000	12,000
Equipment	1,000	900
Stock	5,000	4,500
Debtors	2,250	2,000
Bank	1,000	1,200
Creditors	2,000	2,300

Feedback

4.7 Your balance sheet should look like this:

Balance Sheet as at 31 December 19X1

	£	£	£
Fixed assets			
Premises			12,000
Equipment			1,000
			13,000
Current assets			
Stock	5,000		
Debtors	2,250		
Bank	1,000		
		8,250	
Less current liabilities			
Creditors		2,000	
			6,250
			19,250
Capital			19,250

Balance Sheet as at 31 December 19X2

	£	£	£
Fixed assets			
Premises			12,000
Equipment			900
			12,900
Current assets			
Stock	4,500		
Debtors	2,000		
Bank	1,200		
		7,700	
Current liabilities			
Creditors		2,300	
Working capital			5,400
			18,300
Opening capital 1 January 19X2			19,250
Net loss			(950)
Closing capital 31 December 19X2			18,300

4.8 The trading profit and loss account for 19X2 can be drawn up with just a little bit more information, the bank account providing a lot of detail.

4.9 Now let's use the same example but add the summary of the bank account.

Bank summary at 31 December 19X2

	£		£
Opening balance	1,000	Payments to suppliers	1,500
Cash sales	2,700	Rates	450
Proceed from credit sales	1,750	Wages	2,300
		Closing balance	1,200
	5,450		5,450

4.10 Working from the bank summary:

	£	£
Sales		
Cash		2,700
Credit		1,750
Cash received		4,450
Less opening debtors		2,250
		2,200
Add closing debtors		2,000
		4,200
Expenses		
Rates	450	
Wages	2,300	
	2,750	

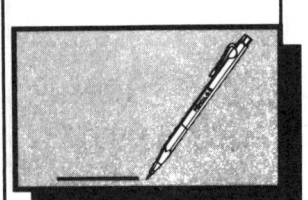

Student Activity 3

Use the bank summary and information above to calculate the purchases figure.

Feedback

4.11 As sales were calculated by taking the cash and bank figures and making adjustments for debtors, purchases are calculated in a similar way. In this case, payments are included with adjustments for creditors.

4.12 Remember that debtors and creditors outstanding at the end of last year relate to sales and purchases in the last year and income from and payments to these relate to the previous year. These sums must be deducted from the cash and bank figures in the bank summary. But debtors and creditors outstanding at the end of the current year relate to this year and must be added to arrive at the sales and purchases figures for the year.

4.13 People often make errors because they do not fully understand this point. Make sure you are happy with it before moving on.

4.14 The calculation is as follows:

	£
Purchases	
Payments	1,500
Less opening creditors	2,000
	(500)
Add closing creditors	2,300
	1,800

4.15 Depreciation does not appear in the bank summary and needs to be calculated separately. In this case:

Depreciation = 100

Bringing the calculations together, we can draw up the trading, profit and loss account.

Trading, profit and loss account for the year ended 31 December 19X2

	£	£
Sales		4,200
Opening stock	5,000	
Add Purchases	<u>1,800</u>	
	6,800	
Less Closing stock	<u>4,500</u>	
Cost of goods sold		<u>2,300</u>
Gross profit		1,900
Less expenses		
Rates	450	
Wages	2,300	
Depreciation	<u>100</u>	
		<u>2,850</u>
Net loss		(950)

4.17 You have now seen how a trading, profit and loss account and balance sheet can be drawn up from incomplete records.

5 Incomplete records

5.1 You may wonder why it is wrong simply to take the figure in the bank account as being the true figure for that year. The reason is given below.

5.2 Let us suppose that on 31 December one year (Year 1) I owe you 100 for goods I bought during the year. This will show on my balance sheet as an accrual of 100 to creditors.

5.3 Next year (Year 2) I pay you 600 from my bank account payments to creditors. Now, how much have I bought from you this year? Not 600 worth of stock, as appears in the bank account, because 100 of that was for last year's goods. To be accurate, my purchases for Year 2 should be shown as 600 - 100 (owed from Year 1) = 500. Take this one stage further. Suppose I now work out that at the end of Year 2 I still owe you 200 for goods I bought during that year. How much have I bought altogether? 500 (actually paid) plus 200 (accrued) = 700.

5.4 Put this together in one sum:

	£
Cash paid	600
Less accrued (from Year 1)	<u>100</u>
	500
Plus accrued (Year 2)	<u>200</u>
True figure for the year	<u>700</u>

5.5 This is probably the most important part of incomplete records you need to know for your exam, because this is where you will earn most of your marks. Suitably adjusted it can be used to work out all sorts of true figures: sales, purchases, rent, rates, heat, etc. anything where you see an opening or a closing balance in the question.

5.6 **Tip**: Sometimes an examiner will give you percentages for profits, either mark up (percentage profit on purchases) or margin (percentage profit on sales), and you will need to use this information to work on the trading, profit and loss account. It is amazing what you can work out from very little information if you use the trading account formula.

	£	£
Sales		xxx
Opening stock	xxx	
Add Purchases	xxx	
Stock available	xxx	
Less Closing stock	xxx	
= Cost of goods sold		xxx
Gross profit		xxx

5.7 As an example:

Jones provides you with the following information:

Opening stock 5,000
Closing stock 6,000
Sales   12,000
Profits are 50% of cost of goods sold.

What are his purchases? Try to work this out before going on to the explanation.

Using the trading account formula, let us fill in what we can so far:

Trading a/c of Jones

	£	£
Sales		12,000
Opening stock	5,000	
Purchases	?	
Less Closing stock	6,000	
Cost of goods sold		
Gross profit		—

5.8 Not much to be going on with, is it?

5.9 The first thing must be to establish profits because we have no information on purchases. What do we know about profits?

5.10 They are 50 per cent of cost of goods sold. How does this help? If we convert that to a fraction it is $\frac{1}{2}$. Now profit on 1 being $\frac{1}{2}$ the selling price must be $1\frac{1}{2}$. Therefore the profit on selling price must be $\frac{1}{3}$. Pictorially this can be represented as

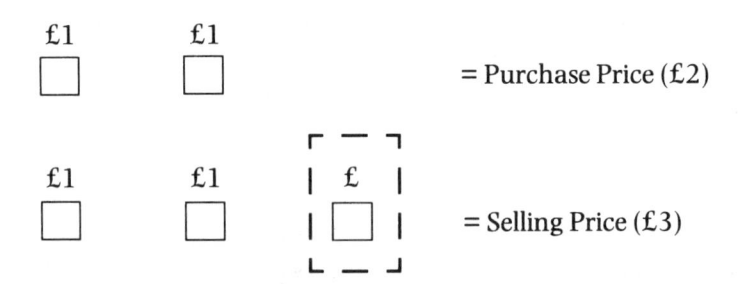

£1 □	£1 □		= Purchase Price (£2)
£1 □	£1 □	⌐ £ ⌐ □ ⌐ ⌐	= Selling Price (£3)

Profit element

5.11 Put the profit element over the purchase price and you have $\frac{1}{2}$ or 50 per cent. Put the profit element over the sales price and you have $\frac{1}{3}$ or $33\frac{1}{3}$ per cent. The difference arises because the selling price includes the element of profit but the purchase price does not.

5.12 This trick applies for any whole fraction. To go from selling price to purchase price deduct one from the denominator; to go from the purchase price add one to the denominator.

Purchase price		**Selling price**
$\frac{1}{2}$	± 1	$\frac{1}{3}$
$\frac{1}{3}$	± 1	$\frac{1}{4}$
$\frac{1}{4}$	± 1	$\frac{1}{5}$
$\frac{1}{5}$	± 1	$\frac{1}{6}$

5.13 So now we can see that the profit in our example must be one-third of the selling price. If we put that in we can then work back up the trading account.

Trading a/c

	£	£
Sales		12,000
Opening stock	5,000	
Purchases(d)	9,000	
Stock available(c)	14,000	
Closing stock	6,000	
Cost of goods sold(b)		8,000
Gross profit(a)		4,000

Notes:

(a) Gross profit is $\frac{1}{3}$ of sales therefore 12,000 x $\frac{1}{3}$ = 4,000.

(b) Cost of goods sold is the difference between sales (12,000) and gross profit (4,000).

(c) Total stock available must be cost of goods sold (8,000) plus closing stock (6,000).

(d) Therefore the purchases figure will be the total of stock available (14,000) less the opening stock (5,000).

5.14 We have spent some time on this topic as nearly every exam contains some element of incomplete records, even if not a whole question. It will pay you to make sure you understand the methods and also to try some more examples if you have the recommended text book.

5.15 As a final exercise and to conclude this Unit, you can put all that you have learned into practice in drawing up the accounts from incomplete records. Write your answer on separate sheets of paper.

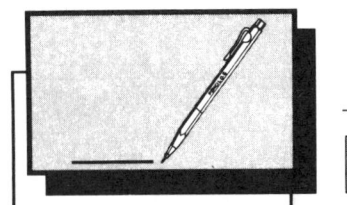

Student Activity 4

Complete the first year's balance sheet, then the trading profit and loss account and balance sheet for the second year, for J. Zajac

31 December 19X2
Sales 20,000 all by cheque
Suppliers paid 14,000 by cheque
Rent 500 by cheque
Wages 1,000 by cheque
Drawings 25 per week by cheque
Debtors repaid 500 by cheque; creditors paid 1,000 by cheque

	19X1	19X2
Debtors	2,200	2,600
Creditors	800	1,500
Bank	2,150	4,850
Stock	3,000	4,200

Fixed assets: The only fixed asset is equipment valued at 2,000 on 31 December 19X1, depreciated by 400 per annum.

Feedback

5.16 Check your accounts against these:

J. Zajac
Balance sheet as at 31 December 19X1

	£	£	£
Fixed assets			
Equipment			2,000
Current assets			
Stock		3,000	
Debtors		2,200	
Bank		<u>2,150</u>	
		7,350	
Less current liabilities			
Creditors		<u>800</u>	
Working capital			<u>6,550</u>
			<u>8,550</u>
Capital			<u>8,550</u>

Bank summary

Opening balance	2,150	Suppliers	14,000
Cash sales	20,000	Rent	500
Received from debtors	500	Wages	1,000
		Drawings	1,300
		Creditors paid	1,000
		Closing balance	4,850
	22,650		22,650

Sales

Cash		20,000
Credit		500
		20,500
Less opening debtors		2,200
		18,300
Add closing debtors		2,600
		20,900

Expenses

Rent	500	
Wages	1,000	
	1,500	

Purchases

Payments:	Cash		14,000
	Credit		1,000
			15,000
Less opening creditors			800
			14,200
Add closing creditors			1,500
			15,700

Depreciation   400

J. Zajac
Trading profit and loss account for the year ended 31 December 19X2

	£	£
Sales		20,900
Opening stock	3,000	
Purchases	15,700	
	18,700	
Closing stock	4,200	
Cost of goods sold		14,500
Gross profit		6,400
Less expenses		
Rent	500	
Wages	1,000	
Depreciation	400	
		1,900
Net profit		4,500

J. Zajac
Balance sheet as at 31 December 19X2

	£	£	£
Fixed assets	Cost	Dep.	NBV
Equipment	2,000	400	1,600
Current assets			
Stock	4,200		
Debtors	2,600		
Bank	4,850		
		11,650	
Current liabilities			
Creditors		1,500	
Working capital			10,150
			11,750
Capital			8,550
Add Net profit			4,500
			13,050
Less Drawings			1,300
			11,750

5.17 If your balance sheet didn't balance straight away, you should have looked back to find your error(s). Remember the golden rule the balance sheet must balance!

5.18 **Tip**: in an exam, if your balance sheet does not balance do not spend time looking for the difference. That time can be better spent earning marks on the next question. Go back to find errors only if you have time once you have completed all the other questions.

6 Summary

6.1 You now know what incomplete records are and how, despite limited information, you can still draw up the accounts. In this Unit you have used knowledge you already had about the trading profit and loss account and the balance sheet, and expanded on it.

6.2 You saw how the capital can be calculated as the total assets less liabilities, and that the profit for the year is the difference between the relative capitals of two years.

6.3 And, with a bank summary and figures for debtors and creditors, the sales and purchases can be calculated for inclusion in the trading account.

7 Self-assessment questions

1. What are incomplete records?

2. Why are incomplete records relatively common in small businesses?

3. What is the balance sheet equation?

4. How can the net profit for the year of a business be estimated if you only have details of assets and liabilities for two consecutive years?

5. If sales are 15,000, and gross profit is 1/3 of sales, what figure should be included in the account for purchases?

6. From the following, calculate the sales figure:

    - Opening debtors   15,000
    - Cash received from debtors 42,000
    - Closing debtors   12,000

7. From the following, calculate the purchase figure:

    - Opening creditors   12,000
    - Payments to creditors 79,000
    - Closing creditors   27,000

8. Explain how you would deal with accrued rent due at the end of each year in calculating the rent figure for inclusion in the profit and loss account.

9. The payment for insurance in the bank account of a business for the financial year was 1,500. 100 was accrued due at the start of the year and 200 was prepaid at the end of the year. What would be the insurance figure that will appear in the profit and loss account?

10. Name two entries, other than accruals and prepayments, which may need to be calculated in the profit and loss account which do not feature in the bank account.

Unit 9

Cash Flow Statements

Objectives

At the end of this Unit you will be able to:
- **define the purpose of the cash flow statement**
- **identify inflows of cash**
- **identify outflows of cash**
- **draw up a cash flow statement as per the requirements of FRS 1.**

1 Introduction

1.1 So far we have looked at the trading and profit and loss account. These give us the profit figures, which are a good indication of performance. These lead on to the balance sheet, which brings together all the outstanding assets and liabilities at the balance sheet date.

1.2 During the year, fixed and current assets are purchased and sold, liabilities are paid back and new loans and capital may be obtained. A way of showing these movements is to draw up a cash flow statement and this is the topic we shall look at in this Unit. Our concentration will be on cash and cash movements.

2 Why is cash flow important?

2.1 A company needs cash flowing through the business, otherwise it would be unable to pay its debts as they fall due, even if it is able to sell goods at a profit. Without sufficient funds a company would grind to a halt.

2.2 Companies publish a trading, profit and loss account and balance sheet which may show a profit, but to the majority of readers it may hide a cash flow problem.

2.3 Financial Reporting Standard, Number 1 (FRS 1), makes it obligatory for all businesses to publish a cash flow statement that shows where funds have come from and where they are going. This will provide the reader with an indication of the company's financial policy and its overall effect on the company's financial position.

2.4 The main objective of this statement is for companies to report their cash inflow and outflow for a period on a standard basis. FRS 1 requires this information to be presented under five standard headings, as shown below.

1 Operating activities
This must show:

- Net profit before tax and interest

- *add* back depreciation for the year (this is a non-cash item)

    less gain on sale of fixed asset or *plus* loss on sale of fixed asset

- *plus or minus* any changes in working capital (stock, debtors and creditors only).

2 Returns on investment and servicing of finance
This must show:

- interest paid (outflow)

- interest received (inflow)

- dividends paid (outflow)

- dividends received (inflow).

3 Taxation
This must show:

- corporation tax paid during the year.

4 Investing activities
This must show:

- purchase of fixed asset (outflow)

- sale of fixed assets (inflow).

5 Financing activities
This must show:

- shares issued (inflow)

- long-term loans received (inflow)

- long-term loans repaid (outflow).

2.5 The total of the sections is then matched with the changes in bank/cash during the year.

2.6 We'll look at some of these items and try to understand what is required.

1   Changes in working capital

2.7   To be able to calculate the changes in the working capital we must compare two balance sheets and look at the increases and decreases that have taken place over the year and ascertain whether these have increased or decreased the bank/cash balance.

	19X3 £		19X4 £
Current assets		*Current assets*	
Stock	20,000	Stock	25,000
Debtors	15,000	Debtors	16,000
Current liabilities		*Current liabilities*	
Creditors	14,000	Creditors	15,000

2.8   As you can see from this example, stock has increased by £5,000, i.e. we have spent £5,000 more on stock this year. This will result in an outflow of funds, and will appear as (5,000) in the statement.

2.9   Debtors have increased by £1,000; this will result in a decrease in the funds available and will appear as (1,000) in the statement.

2.10   Creditors have increased by £1,000; this will result in more funds being available in the short term and will be +1,000 in the statement.

Student Activity 1

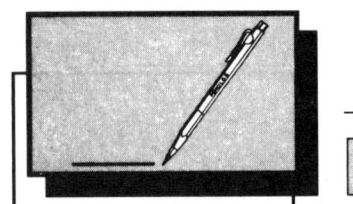

From the following, state whether there is an increase or decrease in each item, and the effect it will have on the cash flow statement (+ or -).

	19X3		19X4
	£		£
Current assets		*Current assets*	
Stock	20,000	Stock	21,000
Debtors	15,000	Debtors	14,000
Current liabilities		*Current liabilities*	
Creditors	14,000	Creditors	12,000

Stock:

Debtors:

Creditors:

Feedback

2.11 Stock has increased by £1,000, therefore there will be (1,000) outflow of cash.

2.12 Debtors have decreased by £1,000, therefore +1,000 inflow of cash.

2.13 Creditors have decreased by £2,000, therefore (2,000) outflow of cash.

2 Dividends paid

2.14 This is dividends paid not proposed; always take the previous year's figures from the balance sheet.

3 Corporation tax

2.15 Again this is what has been paid; look at the previous year's figures for this Tax.

2.16 Both dividends paid and corporation tax will be found under current liabilities on the balance sheet

4 Purchase and sale of fixed assets

2.17 Look at the balance sheets and make comparisons; have the fixed assets changed? Also read any attached notes to the accounts.

5 Shares and loans

2.18 Look at the balance sheets and look at any changes in shares issued together with any long-term loans that may have been increased or decreased.

2.19 Remember – **Look and compare**!

2.20 When you are asked to complete a cash flow statement, it is a good idea to look at the changes in cash and bank first, as this is straightforward and gives you something to work from.

3 Layout of cash flow statement

3.1 The following shows the layout of a cash flow statement:

A Trader Company
Cash flow Statement for the year ended 30 June 19X2

	£	£
Operating activities		
Net profit before tax and interest	xx	
+ depreciation for year	xx	
+ loss or - profit on fixed asset	xx	
Increase/decrease in stocks	xx	
Increase/decrease in debtors	xx	
Increase/decrease in creditors	xx	
Net cash inflow from operating activities		xx
Returns in investment and servicing of finance		
- Interest paid	xx	
+ Interest received	xx	
- Dividends paid	xx	
		xx
Taxation		
- Tax paid		xx
Investing activities		
- Purchase of fixed assets	xx	
+ Sale of fixed assets	xx	
Net cash in/outflow from investment activities	xx	
Net cash in/outflow before financing		xx
Financing		
+ New shares issued	xx	
+ New loans taken	xx	
- Loans repaid	xx	
		xx
Increase/decrease in cash/bank		xx
Analysis of changes in cash and bank		xx

4 How to draw up a cash flow statement

4.1 The following is typical of the information we need to draw up a cash flow statement.

A Trader
Balance sheet as at 31 December 19X1

	19X1			19X2		
	£	£	£	£	£	£
Fixed assets	Cost	Dep.	NBV	Cost	Dep.	NBV
Premises	6,000	–	6,000	6,000	–	6,000
Equipment	–	–	–	5,000	1,000	4,000
	6,000	–	6,000	11,000	1,000	10,000
Current assets						
Stock	2,500			3,900		
Debtors	1,000			2,200		
Bank	200			700		
		3,700			6,800	
Less current liabilities						
Creditors		3,200			3,800	
Working capital			500			3,000
			6,500			13,000
Less long-term liabilities						
Loan			–			3,000
			6,500			10,000
Capital			5,000			6,500
Net profit			1,500			3,500
			6,500			10,000

4.2   From this we can then move on to the cash flow statement:

A Trader
Cash flow statement for year ended 31 December 19X2

	£	£
Operating activities		
Net profit		3,500
Add depreciation for year		<u>1,000</u>
		4,500
Increase in stock	(1,400)	
Increase in debtors	(1,200)	
Increase in creditors	<u>600</u>	
		<u>(2,000)</u>
Net cash flow from operating activities		2,500
Investing activities		
Purchase of fixed assets		<u>(5,000)</u>
Net cash outflow before financing		(2,500)
Financing		
Long-term loan		3,000
Increase in bank		500*
Analysis of changes in bank		
Balance at 31 December 19X1	200	
Balance at 31 December 19X2	<u>700</u>	
Net cash inflow		500*

* These two figures should always balance.

4.3   NB If a sole trader has taken some drawings this should be shown under the heading of returns on investment and servicing of finance.

Student Activity 2

Draw up a cash flow statement for the year ending 31 December 19X5. Write your answer on separate sheets of paper.

Remember – look and compare.

Mrs Jones – A Business Ltd
Balance sheet as at 31 December 19X1

	19X4				19X5	
	£	£	£	£	£	£
Fixed assets	Cost	Dep.	NBV	Cost	Dep.	NBV
Shop fittings	1,500	500	1,000	2,000	750	1,250
Current assets						
Stock		3,750			4,850	
Debtors		625			1,040	
Bank		220				
		4,595			5,890	
Current liabilities						
Creditors	2,020			4,360		
Bank overdraft				725		
		2,020			5,085	
Working capital			2,575			805
Net assets			3,575			2,055
Less: Long-term loan			–			1,000
			3,575			1,055
Financed by:						
Capital			3,300			3,575
Net profit			5,450			4,080
			8,750			7,655
Less drawings			5,175			6,600
			3,575			1,055

8

Feedback

4.4 Your cash flow statement should agree with ours

Mrs Jones
Cash flow statement for year ending 31 December 19X2

	£	£
Operating activities		
Net profit		4,080
Add Depreciation for year		250
		4,330
Increase in stock	(1,100)	
Increase in debtors	(415)	
Increase in creditors	2,340	
		825
Net cash inflow from operating activities		5,155
Returns of investment and servicing of finance		
Drawings		(6,600)
		(1,145)
Investing activities		
Purchase of fixed asset		(500)
Net cash **outflow** before financing		(1,945)
Financing		
Loan		1,000
Decrease in bank		(945)
Analysis of change:		
Balance 31 December 19X4	220	
Balance 31 December 19X5	(725)	
Net cash outflow:	(945)	

5 Cash flow statements for limited companies

5.1 So far we have compiled cash flows that have been fairly straightforward and the net profit has been easy to calculate. With limited companies it is necessary to recalculate the net profit figure making some adjustments for payment of tax and dividends, as well as any transfers to reserves.

5.2 The best way to do this is to follow these steps:

1 Take the last year's retained profit/loss figure from this year's retained profit/loss figure.

2 Add back this year's taxation figure.

3 Add back this year's proposed dividends.

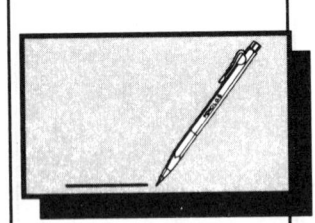

4   Add back any transfers to reserves.

5.3   This will then give you the operating profit.

Student Activity 3

From the following balance sheet extracts, calculate the operating profit.

	19X0 £	19X1 £
Shares and reserves		
Share capital	200,000	220,000
General reserve	15,000	20,000
Retained profit/loss	175,000	200,000
Current liabilities		
Taxation	10,000	12,000
Proposed dividends	20,000	30,000

Feedback

5.4   Your calculations should agree with this:

	£
Retained profit (200 - 175)	25,000
Add back taxation (19X1)	12,000
Add back dividends (19X1)	30,000
Add back transfer to general reserve (20 - 15)	5,000
Operating profit	72,000

(This figure would be transferred to the cash flow statement.)

5.5 Now work through this example of a company's cash flow statement.

Toonsville
Balance sheet as at 31 December 19X4

	19X3			19X4		
	£	£	£	£	£	£
Fixed assets	Cost	Dep.	NBV	Cost	Dep.	NBV
Various	47,200	6,200	41,000	64,000	8,900	55,100
Current assets						
Stock		7,000			11,000	
Debtors		5,000			3,900	
Bank		1,000			300	
		13,000			15,200	
Current liabilities						
Creditors	3,500			4,800		
Proposed dividends	2,000			2,500		
Corporation tax	1,000			1,500		
		6,500			8,800	
Working capital			6,500			6,400
Net assets			47,500			61,500
Less: Long-term liabilities						
Debentures			5,000			3,000
			42,500			58,500
Financed by:						
Ordinary share capital			30,000			40,000
Share premium A/c			1,500			2,500
Retained profits			11,000			16,000
			42,500			58,500

5.6 Firstly we must work out the net profit using the same procedure as in activity 3.

	£	£
Retained profit	(16,000 -11,000)	5,000
Add back tax		1,500
Add back dividends		
Operating profit - transfer this figure to the cash flow statement		9,000

Cash flow statement for the year ending 31 December 19X4

	£	£
Operating profit		9,000
Add Depreciation (8,900 - 6,200)		2,700
		11,700
Increase in stock	(4,000)	
Decrease in debtors	1,100	
Increase in creditors	1,300	
		(1,600)
		10,100
Returns on investment and servicing of finance		
Dividends paid		(2,000)
		8,100
Taxation paid		(1,000)
		7,100
Investing activities		
Purchase of fixed assets (64,000 - 47,200)		(16,800)
Net cash outflow before financing		(9,700)
Financing		
Issue of shares at a premium (10,000 + 1,000)	11,000	
Repayment of debentures	(2,000)	(9,000)
Net cash outflow:		(700)
Changes in bank balance		
19X3	1,000	
19X4	300	
Decrease	(700)	

5.7 Now try activity 4.

Student Activity 4

This question is more complex and will require you to look very carefully at each balance sheet to compare the various items.

Prepare Pickering plc's cash flow statement for 31 December 19X2. Use separate paper.

Balance sheet for Pickering plc

	19X1			19X2		
	£	£	£	£	£	£
	Cost	Dep.	NBV	Cost	Dep.	NBV
Fixed assets	212,000	10,000	202,000	365,000	20,000	345,000

Current assets				
Stock	36,000		40,000	
Debtors	29,700		17,000	
Cash	100		1,000	
		65,800		58,000

Less current liabilities				
Creditors	30,000		40,000	
Tax	12,000		21,000	
Dividends	8,000		15,000	
Bank Overdraft	2,000		45,000	
	52,000		121,000	
Working capital		13,800		(63,000)
		215,800		282,000
Less: Long-term liabilities				
Debentures		10,000		30,000
		205,800		252,000
Shares and reserves				
Share capital		150,000		175,000
General reserve		20,000		25,000
Profit and loss account		35,800		52,000
		205,800		252,000

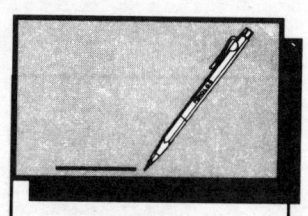

Feeback

5.8 Your cash flow statement should look like this:

Pickering plc
Cash flow statement for year ending 31 December 19X2

	£	£
Operating activities		
Net profit before tax and interest (see note)	57,200	
Add depreciation	10,000	
	67,200	
Increase in stocks	(4,000)	
Decrease in debtors	12,700	
Increase in creditors	10,000	
		18,700
Net cash flow from operating activities		85,900
Returns on investment and servicing of finance		
Dividends paid		(8,000)
		77,900
Taxation		(12,000)
Taxation paid		65,900
Investing activities		
Purchase of fixed assets		(153,000)
Net cash outflow from investing activities		(87,100)
Financing		
Issue of shares		25,000
Debentures		20,000
Decrease in bank/cash		(42,100)

Analysis of bank and cash

	Cash	Bank	
Balance 31 December 19X1	100	(2,000)	
Balance 31 December 19X2	1,000	(45,000)	
Change	900	(43,000)	
Overall change			(42,100)

Note:

Difference in profit/loss balance	16,200
Add back taxation	21,000
Add back proposed dividends	15,000
Add back transfer to general reserve	5,000
	57,200

6 Summary

6.1 In this Unit you saw that FRS 1 makes it obligatory for many businesses to publish a cash flow statement. This statement shows where all funds have come from and where they have gone.

6.2 The following are examples of sources of cash: Profits, sales of fixed assets, issues of shares, long-term borrowing (loans, debentures).

6.3 Applications of cash may include: Losses; purchase of fixed assets, repayment of loans, payment of tax and dividends.

6.4 In addition to cash movements, an adjustment has to be made for depreciation, as this is a non-cash item.

6.5 If you have to recalculate the net profit remember to make adjustments for tax, dividends and any transfers to reserves.

6.6 Remember the layout and all headings:

Operating activities
Returns on investment and financing
Taxation
Investing activities
Financing.

6.7 The cash flow statement provides an indication of the financial policy of a company and how a company finances its long-term investments.

7 Self-assessment questions

1. What is FRS 1?

2. List the five standard headings in a cash flow statement.

3. State the items that might be found in returns on investment and servicing of finance.

4. What corporation tax figure do we use in the cash flow statement?

5. What does the cash flow statement show?

6. What is meant by changes in working capital?

7. How would you deal with proposed and paid dividends in a cash flow statement?

8. How are shares and loans included in a cash flow statement?

9. How would you deal with depreciation in a cash flow statement?

10. What adjustments would you expect to make if you have to recalculate profit?

17

Unit 10
Costing

> **Objectives**
>
> At the end of this Unit you will be able to:
> - define fixed and variable costs
> - define direct and indirect costs
> - carry out a break even analysis
> - explain the use of projected costings in decision-making.

1 Introduction

1.1 Most of the areas we have considered so far have been concerned with recording results and with historical information. This is useful but when businesses are looking to make decisions, they need to look forward.

1.2 Some typical decisions involve prices and costs of goods and services and it is such matters that we will turn to now. First of all we will look at the basic differences between types of cost.

2 Fixed costs

2.1 These are the costs which have to be paid regardless of the level of output. They include items like rent and rates on the business premises, which must be paid. As well as these costs, if depreciation is on a straight-line basis then this cost is incurred even if the equipment or vehicles to which it relates are not working at full capacity, or not working at all in the event of annual holidays which necessitate a factory shut-down.

3 Variable costs

3.1 Variable costs, unlike fixed costs, are related to the level of output. If production is low, less materials will be bought in and the wage bill may be lower if a bonus scheme is operated.

3.2 Items such as heating and lighting can fall somewhere between the two types of cost, as they would have to be used if some production were taking place, making them a fixed cost. But if part of the factory were not being used, for example because of annual holidays, then these costs would be classified as variable. It really depends on the individual business as to whether such items can be considered fixed or variable costs; views differ. As long as you understand the principle, then you can make this judgement.

3.3 The effect of these costs on a new project can be vital.

3.4 Work through the following example

New equipment is required to increase production to meet a prospective output of 100,000 units; the current output is 50,000 units. Sale price per unit is 10.

Costs	£
Factory rent	7,500
New equipment leased	5,000 per year
Raw material per unit	1.00
Labour costs per unit	2.00
Variable costs per unit	1.50
Fixed costs	5,000

Required:

Profit forecast on the present 50,000 and the projected 100,000 units with the new equipment.

The above information gives us the following. We will start by showing the workings for the different classes of cost.

	50,000 units		100,000 units	
	£	£	£	£
Sales		50,000		100,000
Fixed costs				
Rent	7,500		7,500	
Equipment	–		5,000	
	7,500		12,500	
Variable costs				
Raw materials		50,000		100,000
Labour		100,000		200,000
Other variable costs		75,000		150,000
		225,000		450,000
Fixed costs		7,500		12,500
Add variable costs		225,000		450,000
		232,500		462,500
Sales		500,000		1,000,000
Less costs		232,500		462,500
Profit		267,500		537,500

3.5 In this example the increase in profit is reflected by the increased output and it could be worth investing the extra money. If the fixed costs were a lot higher then the increase in profits would be much greater.

4 Direct and indirect costs

4.1 Direct costs are those which can directly be related to individual units of the business. That is, the costs are only related to that unit and as such it can be treated as a cost centre.

4.2 Indirect costs are those which are not directly related to one unit but are shared by several.

4.3 Let us say that in a factory there are two units which produce different goods. The direct costs are those which relate to the individual production lines, but the factory rent, rates and maybe even heating and lighting are not directly related to the individual units. Therefore, these indirect costs must be shared between the two units.

4.4 When assessing the profitability of the individual units some care must be exercised. If one unit is losing money then shutting this down will not necessarily make the business more profitable because the poor performing unit is contributing to the indirect costs.

5 Break even analysis

5.1 A break even analysis is often undertaken and particularly so when a new project is being considered. The break even point is when the sales contributions are equal to the fixed costs. This can be expressed as:

$$\text{Break even} = \frac{\text{Fixed Costs}}{\text{Contribution per unit}}$$

5.2 It is also often shown as a graph. See Figure 10.1

Figure 10.1: Break even

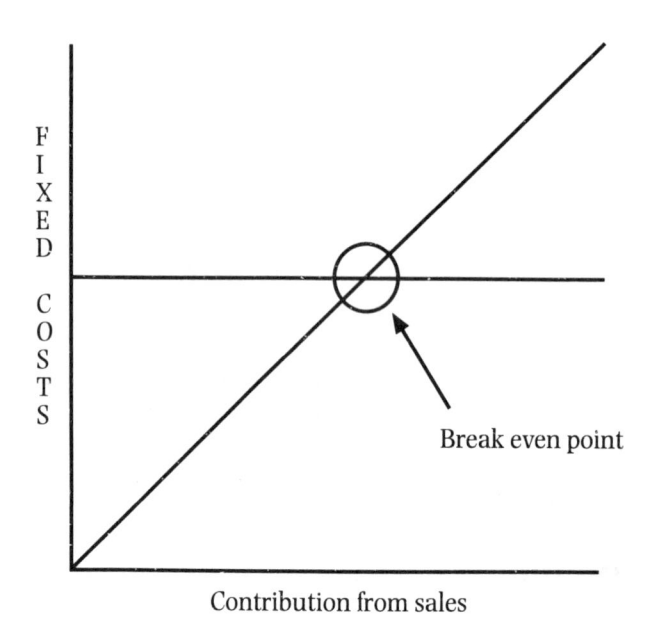

Student Activity 1

Take a look at the graph in Figure 10.1. Contribution is calculated as sales income less variable costs. It is called contribution because each unit sold where there is an excess of income above variable costs makes a contribution towards paying off fixed costs. What is the significance of the break even point?

Feedback

5.3   You should have noticed that below the break even point the business is making a loss; above this point it is making a profit. So a business will want to know its break even point so that it can assess the level of sales it needs to make before it can start making a profit on a particular product.

6   Margin of Safety

6.1   The margin of safety is the amount by which forecast sales exceed the break even point.

e.g.   Break even point   =   1000 units
        Forecast sales   =   2000 units

        Margin of safety   =   1000 units 50%

6.2 Work through the following example

Costs

Fixed costs	£25,000
Variable costs per unit	£2.00
Selling price per unit	£6.00

To calculate the break even point, you must first establish the contribution per unit.

£6.00-£2.00 = 4 contribution

So break even point = $\dfrac{25{,}000}{4}$ = 6,250 units

Below 6,250 units a loss is made but above it the business will make a profit.

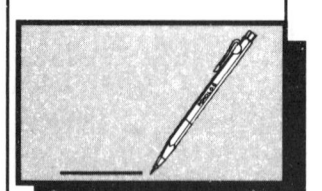

Student Activity 2

Calculate the break even point from the following:-

Costs

Fixed costs	50,000
Variable costs per unit	5.00
Selling price per unit	10.00

Feedback

6.3 Your calculation should agree with this:

Contribution = £10.00-£5.00
5 per unit

Fixed costs = $\dfrac{50{,}000}{5}$

Contribution per unit:

Break even point = 10,000 units

Student Activity 3

Calculate the break even point and the profit at 20,000 and 50,000 units for each of these two projects, which involve buying new equipment. Depreciation is by straight-line over five years.

Costs

	Project 1	Project 2
Equipment	15,000	25,000
Fixed costs	5,000	5,000
Variable costs per unit	5.00	8.00
Selling price per unit	10.00	10.00

Feedback

6.4   Your calculation should agree with this:

	Project 1	Project 2
Contribution	£10.00 - £5.00 = £5	£10.00 - £8.00 = £2
Break even point	= 1,600 units	= 5,000 units
At 20,000 units		
Contribution	£100,000	£40,000
Fixed costs	£8,000	£10,000
	£92,000	£30,000
At 50,000 units		
Contribution	£250,000	£100,000
Fixed costs	£8,000	£10,000
	£242,000	£90,000

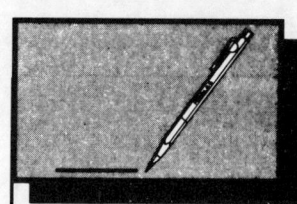

6.5 It is quite clear at both production levels that project 1 has a more profitable outcome with a lower investment in the fixed costs.

7 Contribution costing

7.1 Contribution costing assumes that the contribution from a unit first goes to meet its variable costs and then any remaining contribution goes towards the fixed costs. Beyond the fixed costs coverage the residue adds to the profit for each unit sold.

8 Target profit calculation

8.1 This method gives the number of units or value to meet a required profit. It assumes that there is sufficient contribution to meet the fixed costs so that the residue goes to the profit.

8.2 It is expressed as follows:

$$\text{Units sold} = \frac{\text{Fixed costs} + \text{Desired profit}}{\text{Contribution per unit}}$$

8.3 Work through the following example:

Profit required	£50,000
Fixed costs	£30,000
Variable costs per unit	£5.00
Selling price per unit	£9.00

Contribution

Selling price per unit	£9.00
Less Variable costs per unit	£5.00
Contribution	–

$$\text{Sales required} \quad \frac{30{,}000 + 20{,}000 \text{ units}}{4.00} = \underline{20{,}000} \text{ units}$$

Student Activity 4

Calculate the number of units and value to meet a required profit of 100,000 from the following information:

Costs

Fixed costs	20,000
Variable costs per unit	7.50
Selling price per unit	12.50

Feedback

8.4 Your calculation should agree with this:

Selling price per unit	12.50
Variable costs per unit	7.50
	5.00

$$\text{Sales required} = \frac{20,000 + 100,000}{5.00} = 24,000$$

24,000 units value = 24,000 x 12.50 = 300,000

9 Summary

9.1 You should now understand how different forms of costing work and realise when maybe one or a combination can be utilised. It is important that you appreciate how these different methods work as a decision to start a new project or review an existing one may well be affected by the costing analysis for the overall business.

9.2 Specifically, you have seen that costs can be fixed or variable, direct or indirect. Once you have identified the cost categories, you can use them to calculate contribution per unit and decide on matters such as the break even point for goods and services, the margin of safety and appropriate pricing level.

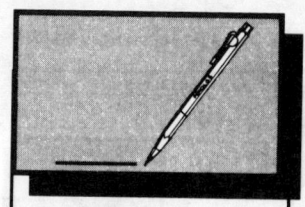

Self-assessment questions

1. Distinguish between fixed and variable cost.

2. Distinguish between direct and indirect cost.

3. A business has the following costs:
   - Annual rent for factory and offices 10,000
   - Annual depreciation of manufacturing plant 6,000
   - Materials per unit 4.20
   - Direct wages per unit 5.50
   - Factory manager's salary 15,000 p.a.

   Which of the above are fixed costs, variable costs, direct costs and indirect costs?

4. What is meant by contribution?

5. A business has the following costs and income:
   - Sales income 7.00 per unit
   - Variable costs per unit 5.00.
   - Fixed costs   20,000

   The business makes 10,000 units per year.

   Calculate the contribution per unit.

6. What is the formula for break even point?

7. Why is it important for a business to know its break even point?

8. What is a margin of safety?

9. What formula is used for the target profit calculation?

10. Calculate the break even point and margin of safety for the following:
    - Sales   100,000 units
    - Fixed costs   300,000
    - Variable cost 8.00 per unit
    - Selling price 14.00 per unit

Unit 11

Budget Forecasts and Cash Flow Forecasts Part I

Objectives

At the end of this Unit you will be able to:

- explain how and why budgets and forecasts are used
- explain how inflation affects the accounts
- define and construct a cash flow forecast.

1 Introduction

1.1 Planning is a very important part of every business from the sole trader to the public limited company. The business needs to know where it is going, and what its plans are for investment, expansion and to increase its profit margin.

1.2 Short, medium and long-term planning is necessary. Long-term plans will look at the overall position the business wants to be in in, say, ten years time; the short and medium-term plans are the means of achieving this overall objective. When this objective is in sight, new long-term plans will be drawn up. So, you see, planning is a continual process.

1.3 The budgets are the short-term plans, broken down by department, so that each unit has a target to work towards. This would be, for example, sales, production of product x, production of y, production of z, marketing, personnel, etc. Each budget must be realistic and all will fit together to meet the overall objective. It is no good having an increase in production which will require more workers if this is not allowed for in the personnel budget from which the wages, and related expenses have to be met. These budgets will usually cover a 12-month period, but may be broken down further to quarterly or monthly budgets. Any significant variance from the budget to the actual results must be investigated to find out what has happened and why. The variance may be a one-off, but then again the budgets may have to be redrawn to reflect this change. It is not altogether unusual for the budgets to be redrawn because all events cannot be foreseen.

1.4 Budgets are therefore part of the planning process, which itself involves forecasting. Nobody can foresee all future events, but forecasting is still useful. A reasonable estimate of the future can be made by using the current data, so you have a base on which to work and from which to project forward. So, if the target was to increase sales by 5 %, as well as all the figures involved in this calculation you must also forecast the projected cost of materials and selling price allowing for inflation. From the forecast the estimated trading profit and loss account and balance sheet can be drawn up as well as cash flow forecasts. In the heading it will state that they are estimated; other than this it is the same as you have looked at already.

2   What is a cash flow forecast?

2.1 A cash flow forecast is an estimation of the amounts of cash to be received and paid. It is concerned only with cash, which in practical terms means the bank account. Any entries that do not involve cash (such as depreciation, which is merely a bookkeeping entry) are not included. The usual time span covered by the forecast is 12 months, although they can be drawn up for shorter or longer periods.

3   Why are cash flow forecasts used?

3.1 By using cash flow forecasts you can examine the implications of the firm's trading on the cash resources of the business. So, for example, you could see what would happen if you extended the existing credit terms. This delay in receiving cash could have some serious consequences for the firm's cash flow (i.e. the money the firm receives and the money it has to pay out). If the timing is not correct, the firm would be short of funds or even run out altogether. A cash flow forecast highlights these critical times for the firm so it can plan accordingly. Although, in the end, these forecasts may not be right, this process is part of the overall planning of the company. By means of a cash flow forecast a company will be better prepared and even have contingency plans ready to implement. It is a very useful exercise to compare the planned results against the actual, to see what happened and why; this will be covered in the next Unit.

Student Activity 1

Sally's business computer needs replacing and a new one would cost 3,000 today. How can she identify when she can afford to buy the computer or estimate how much she needs to borrow to finance the purchase? What does she need to bear in mind if she puts off the purchase for several months?

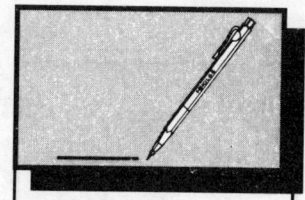

Feedback

3.2 To make this kind of decision, Sally needs to ascertain the amount of cash she has available and what her commitments will be over the next few months. The best way to do this would be to draw up a cash forecast. She might, for instance, check her bank account and find that she has 3,200 in the bank which is sufficient to pay for the computer. But, she might also have a tax bill of 2,000 to pay in a month's time. If she were to write out a cheque now, without considering the future, she could quickly be in trouble.

3.3 A cash flow forecast will show Sally whether she can afford to buy the computer in the next few months and finance it from income or whether she will need to borrow, and how much she will need to borrow. If a cash forecast shows that the minimum balance on her bank account over the next six months is going to be, say, 1,000, Sally may decide that she only has to borrow 2,000 towards the total purchase price.

3.4 Sally can then include the cost of the new computer in her budget for the forthcoming period.

3.5 However, if Sally does not buy the computer immediately, the price may change. Inflation generally causes the prices of goods and services to rise over time and an allowance should be made for inflation if any purchase is deferred. Computers may differ because technological changes mean that the 'top of the range' computer now is likely to be replaced in three months' time. Sally may be able to buy the computer she has in mind now for less in a few months.

3.6 **Tip**: When answering questions of this nature in the examination, show your understanding of what happens in practice. Without thinking, it would be easy in this case to talk about inflation and disregard technological or other factors.

4 How is a cash flow forecast drawn up?

4.1 First, you will need to prepare your estimation of the cash to be received and paid. You will also have to decide what period the forecast is to cover. With this information in hand you will be ready to draw up the cash flow forecast (see Unit 10 for more examples). Look at the following example:

The following is a three-month cash flow forecast, with monthly sales of 1,000 cash and purchases of 500 per month cash.

	Month 1 £	Month 2 £	Month 3 £
Sales	1,000	1,000	1,000
Total receipts	1,000	1,000	1,000
Purchases	500	500	500
Total payments	500	500	500
Cash balance	500	1,000	1,500

4.2 The above is a simple example in which there are only purchases and sales for cash. If we add to it some other expenses that have to be paid wages each month of 100 and an electricity bill in Month 3 of 150 then it would be as follows:

	Month 1 £	Month 2 £	Month 3 £
Sales	1,000	1,000	1,000
Total receipts	1,000	1,000	1,000
Purchases	500	500	500
Wages	100	100	100
Electricity	–	–	150
Total payments	600	600	750
	400	400	250
Cash balance	400	800	1,050

4.3 This still assumes that the cash/bank balance started at nil, but in reality there would already be a balance, either positive or negative. Let us say at the beginning of Month 1 that the balance was 250. The forecast would therefore be drawn up as follows:

	Month 1 £	Month 2 £	Month 3 £
Sales	1,000	1,000	1,000
Total receipts	1,000	1,000	1,000
Purchases	500	500	500
Wages	100	100	100
Electricity			150
Total payments	600	600	750
Bank/cash balance	250	650	1,050
Add receipts	1,000	1,000	1,000
	1,250	1,650	2,050
Less payments	600	600	750
New bank/cash balance	650	1,050	1,300

4.4 This variation on presenting the cash flow forecast is better to use, as it shows the bank/cash balance at the beginning and end of each month.

Student Activity 2

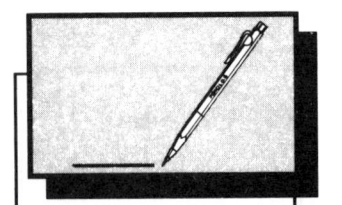

Draw up a cash flow forecast for J. Bingley for three months from the following information:

sales £1,500 per month cash
purchases £700 per month cash
wages £150 per month
rent £100 per month
electricity Month 2 £200
bank balance starts at £200.

Feedback

4.5 Your answer should be as follows. When you first start preparing forecasts and budgets, you may feel a little unsure about the presentation but it will become easier with practice. It takes a little time to draw up these financial statements and it is important to be methodical in your approach.

J. Bingley

	Month 1 £	Month 2 £	Month 3 £
Sales	1,500	1,500	1,500
Total receipts	1,500	1,500	1,500
Purchases	700	700	700
Wages	150	150	150
Rent	100	100	100
Electricity	–	200	–
Total payments	950	1,150	950
Bank balance	200	750	1,100
Add receipts	1,500	1,500	1,500
	1,700	2,250	2,600
Less payments	950	1,150	950
New bank balance	750	1,100	1,650

4.6 You can see that the bank balance has increased month after month.

Student Activity 3

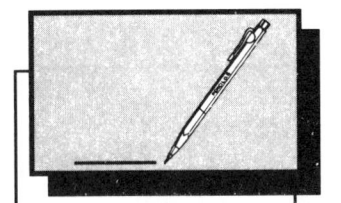

Suppose that J. Bingley sells goods on credit to customers and in Month 2 only half the income from sales is expected (i.e. 750), and also that the rent is increased in Month 3 to 150. Draw up the cash flow forecast for the changed situation over the three month period.

Feedback

4.7 The results of increased expenses and a delay in receiving money from customers reduces the final bank balance for Months 2 and 3. The timing of inflows and outflows of cash are very important for organisations. There are certain expenses, such as wages and salaries, which must be paid on the right date to ensure that the organisation continues to operate. So, cash must be available when it is needed.

4.8 Your answer should be as follows:

J. Bingley

	Month 1 £	Month 2 £	Month 3 £
Sales	1,500	750	1,500
Total receipts	1,500	750	1,500
Purchases	700	700	700
Wages	150	150	150
Rent	100	100	150
Electricity	–	200	–
Total payments	950	1,150	1,000
Bank balance	200	750	350
Add receipts	1,500	750	1,500
	1,700	1,500	1,850
Less payments	950	1,150	1,000
New bank balance	750	350	850

4.9 The major change affecting the bank balance was the delayed income from customers. If this carries on from month to month, the situation can become serious.

Student Activity 4

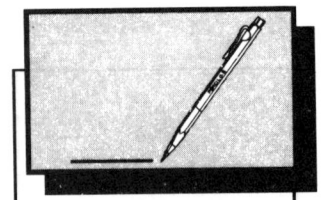

Draw up the cash forecast for J. Bingley for Months 3 and 4 commencing with the opening bank balance of 350 and assuming:

- the other half of Month 2's sales income flow into the business in Month 3

- no income is received in Month 4 because sales made in Month 3 are to be paid for in Months 5 and 6

- all expenses remain at the same level as in the answer to Activity 3 above.

Feedback

4.10 This is more complex than the earlier activities, but again, if you work through the various inflows and outflows carefully, your answer should be as follows. The continued delay in receiving money from customers leads to an overdraft in Month 4. As this is a forecast, action can be taken to avoid the overdraft or an official overdraft limit can be arranged with the bank.

J. Bingley

	Month 3 £	Month 4 £
Sales	750	Nil
Total receipts	750	Nil
Purchases	700	700
Wages	150	150
Rent	150	150
Electricity		
Total payments	1,000	1,000
Bank balance	350	100
Add receipts	750	Nil
	1,100	100
Less payments	1,000	1,000
New bank balance/(overdraft)	100	(900)

4.11 It is conventional in accounting to show negative balances in brackets.

5 Summary

5.1 Planning is important to a business and you have seen in this Unit how this can be translated into forecasts and budgets.

5.2 Forecasts and budgets are useful in the control of organisations because actual results can be compared with them and any variances investigated.

5.3 When preparing forecasts, matters such as sales and expenses are estimates but can be reasonably accurate if based on previous experience. Changing price levels also need to be allowed for in estimates so that proper allowance is made for inflation.

5.4 A cash flow forecast or budget is very important to organisations because difficulties can arise if insufficient cash is available to meet bills when they become due. By anticipating shortages in cash, arrangements can be made for overdrafts or to defer payments. Surplus funds can also be invested.

5.5 You have also drawn up some cash flow forecasts and seen the effects of changes on the bank account, of changes in expenses and changes in timing of receipts and payments. In the next Unit we will expand on these changes and consider their impact.

Self-assessment questions

1. Why do organisations plan?

2. How do budgets help in the planning process?

3. What is meant by a budget variance and how is it dealt with?

4. Explain the purpose of cash flow forecasts.

5. Why is it important to consider inflation when preparing forecasts and budgets?

6. Why is depreciation not shown in a cash flow forecast?

7. Explain the importance of timing in managing cash resources.

8. Briefly explain how the balance in a cash flow forecast alters from one month to the next.

9. Why if, for example, 2,000 of goods are sold in June might only 1,000 be received from customers in June and the remaining 1,000 in July?

10. If the level of sales is expected to increase in a business this will be shown in a cash flow forecast. What other effects will increased sales have on the forecast?

Unit 12

Cash Flow Forecasts Part II

Objectives

At the end of this Unit you will be able to:

- **explain how taking and giving credit affects the cash flow**
- **use the cash flow forecast to assess requests for bank loans and overdrafts.**

1 Introduction

1.1 Having covered the basics of cash flow forecasting, we will now expand on this by taking and giving credit and see how this affects the cash flow. We will also consider how the cash flow forecast can be used in assessing requests for bank loans and overdrafts.

2 The effect of taking credit on the cash flow forecast

2.1 As you know, it is usual for a firm to buy its goods on credit once it is established; this in turn means that the firm has this cash for the credit term. So, if one month's credit is given, and this is not paid until Month 2, in terms of the cash flow forecast in Month 1 there is cash which does not have to be paid out, and in theory it stays in the bank account. Let us see how this works on a three-month forecast.

Bank balance	£100	
Sales	£2,000	per month cash
Purchases	£750	per month taken on one month's credit
Wages	£200	per month
Rent	£150	per month
Rates	£75	per month

| | Month 1 | Month 2 | Month 3 |
	£	£	£
Sales	2,000	2,000	2,000
	2,000	2,000	2,000
Credit purchases	–	750	750
Wages	200	200	200
Rent	150	150	150
Rates	75	75	75
	425	1,175	1,175
Bank balance	100	1,675	2,500
Add receipts	2,000	2,000	2,000
	2,100	3,675	4,500
Less payments	425	1,175	1,175
New bank balance	1,675	2,500	3,325

2.2 This makes quite a bit of difference to the cash available to meet any unexpected commitments.

3 The effect of giving credit on the cash flow forecast

3.1 Just as credit is given to the firm, the firm can, as you know, also give credit to its customers (debtors). The important thing to consider in the terms that are given is the need to have this money already collected before the firm has to pay out to its creditors. If the firm is given one month's credit but gives two months' credit itself, the cash flow will not look very healthy as payments will be made before they can be received from the debtors. The cash flow forecast is the ideal way to highlight this situation. Let us use the same example as before but sell half the goods on two months' credit. The cash flow forecast would be as follows:

	Month 1 £	Month 2 £	Month 3 £
Cash sales	1,000	1,000	1,000
Credit sales	–	–	1,000
	1,000	1,000	2,000
Credit purchases	–	750	750
Wages	200	200	200
Rent	150	150	150
Rates	75	75	75
	425	1,175	1,175
Bank balance	100	675	500
Add receipts	1,000	1,000	2,000
	1,100	1,675	2,500
Less payments	425	1,175	1,175
New bank balance	675	500	1,325

3.2 The bank balance at the end of Month 3 is 2,000 lower because half of the sales were on credit. It would be much better for this firm to take two months' credit and give only one.

Student Activity 1

To see what difference this makes, draw up the new cash flow forecast using the existing figures but changing the credit periods given and taken to one month and two months respectively.

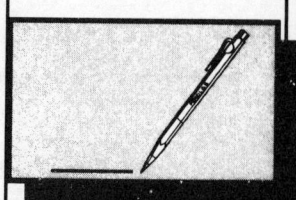

Feedback

	Month 1 £	Month 2 £	Month 3 £
Cash sales	1,000	1,000	1,000
Credit sales	–	1,000	1,000
	1,000	2,000	2,000
Credit purchases	–	–	750
Wages	200	200	200
Rent	150	150	150
Rates	75	75	75
	425	425	1,175
Bank balance	100	675	2,250
Add receipts	1,000	2,000	2,000
	1,100	2,675	4,250
Less payments	425	425	1,175
New bank balance	675	2,250	3,075

3.3 You can see how much better it makes the cash flow just to adjust the period of credit given and taken, and this is of course the preferable and prudent way to do business.

Student Activity 2

Draw up a six-month cash flow forecast (Jan-June) for Your Business from the following information:

Sales	3,500	per month, 1 month's credit
Purchases	1,250	per month, 2 months' credit
Wages	300	per month
Rent	300	per month
Rates	100	per month
Electricity	250	per quarter starting January
Gas	150	per quarter starting February
Telephone	200	per quarter starting January
Postage	50	per month

Bank balance at the beginning of the month 550.

Complete this exercise on a separate paper.

Feedback

3.4 Your cash flow forecast should look like this:

Your Business cash flow forecast January – June 19XX

	Jan £	Feb £	Mar £	Apr £	May £	Jun £
Credit sales	–	3,500	3,500	3,500	3,500	3,500
	–	3,500	3,500	3,500	3,500	3,500
Credit purchases	–	–	1,250	1,250	1,250	1,250
Wages	300	300	300	300	300	300
Rent	300	300	300	300	300	300
Rates	100	100	100	100	100	100
Electricity	250	–	–	250	–	–
Gas	–	150	–	–	150	–
Telephone	200	–	–	200	–	–
Postage	50	50	50	50	50	50
	1,200	900	2,000	2,450	2,150	2,000
Bank balance	550	(650)	1,950	3,450	4,500	5,850
Add receipts	–	3,500	3,500	3,500	3,500	3,500
	550	2,850	5,450	6,950	8,000	9,350
Less payments	1,200	900	2,000	2,450	2,150	2,000
New bank balance	(650)	1,950	3,450	4,500	5,850	7,350

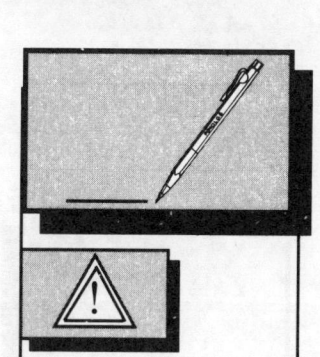

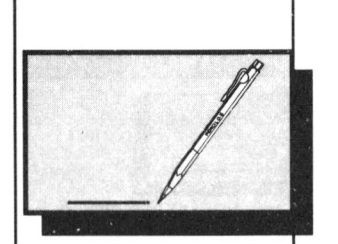

3.5 In this cash flow forecast, because no funds were received in the first month the bank account went overdrawn. From then on with steady sales figures the bank account became very healthy.

Student Activity 3

Use the same figures but reduce the sales in the first three months to 2,000, half sold on credit, and thereafter 3,500, half sold on credit, to draw up the new cash flow forecast.

Draw up this statement on separate paper.

Feedback

3.6 Your new cash flow forecast should look like this:

Your Business cash flow forecast January – June 19XX

	Jan £	Feb £	Mar £	Apr £	May £	Jun £
Cash sales	1,000	1,000	1,000	1,000	1,750	1,750
Credit sales	–	1,000	1,000	1,750	1,750	1,750
	1,000	2,000	2,000	2,750	3,500	3,500
Purchases	–	–	1,250	1,250	1,250	1,250
Wages	300	300	300	300	300	300
Rent	300	300	300	300	300	300
Rates	100	100	100	100	100	100
Electricity	250	–	–	250	–	–
Gas	–	150	–	–	150	–
Telephone	200	–	–	200	–	–
Postage	50	50	50	50	50	50
	1,200	900	2,000	2,450	2,150	2,000
Bank balance	550	350	1,450	1,450	1,750	3,100
Add receipts	1,000	2,000	2,000	2,750	3,500	3,500
	1,550	2,350	3,450	4,200	5,250	6,600
Less payments	1,200	900	2,000	2,450	2,150	2,000
New bank balance	350	1,450	1,450	1,750	3,100	4,600

3.7 Just by adjusting the sales figures at the beginning, we have a positive bank balance at the end of January because half the sales were for cash, but at the end of the day the balance is reduced because of the loss of sales.

4 How the cash flow forecast can be used to assess a bank loan or overdraft

4.1 If a customer comes to the bank with a request for a loan or overdraft the best way to see if this is the right figure and if they can afford to repay it is to draw up a cash flow forecast. You have already seen how apparently small changes can have a significant effect on the cash flow. It is, of course, most important to assess if the forecast is realistic and sometimes the sales will be reduced by, say, 10% by the bank manager to see what effect this has on the overall position. The cash flow forecast would be the same as you have already produced except that there would be monthly repayments and interest charged usually on a quarterly basis.

4.2 It is always a useful activity to compare the forecast with the actual figures, after the expiry of the period for which the cash flow forecast was drawn up. This comparison is drawn up in exactly the same way but using the real figures. If there are significant differences then the question must be asked Why? Were the forecasts unrealistic? Were there some unforeseen circumstances that could not be planned for? Are they likely to happen again? Did the forecast underestimate the sales and/or expenses, and if so why? All these questions must be reasonably answered so that when the next cash flow forecast is drawn up it will be more accurate. This must be part of a continual and ongoing planning process.

Student Activity 4

A request for a loan of 6,000 has been received, repayment over 12 months, to meet some vital repairs which must be paid in January. Draw up the cash flow forecast from the following information for 12 months for B Business.

	£	
Repairs	6,000	
Sales	5,000	$1/_2$ on 2 months' credit
Purchases	3,000	on 3 months' credit
Wages	500	per month
Rent	600	per month
Rates	350	per month
Electricity	1,000	per quarter starting January
Gas	350	per quarter starting January
Telephone	200	per month
Postage	100	per month
Loan repayment	500	per month starting January
Interest	90	per quarter starting March

Bank balance beginning of the month 500.

Draw up your answer on separate paper.

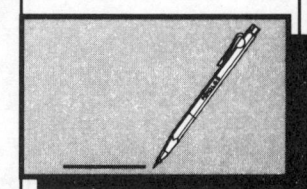

Feedback

4.3　In this case it is clearly unrealistic to try to repay the loan in 12 months without incurring a heavy overdraft. The firm must think again, ensuring that all the other figures are realistic and see if they can repay the loan over 18 or 24 months. If you want some practice, draw up these two cash flow forecasts; we do not give answers. Many situations like this can use the cash flow forecast, to see the implications for the business. It can also be very useful in working out the cash requirements for a firm with seasonal trading, such as makers of Christmas crackers, or firework manufacturers.

5　Summary

5.1　You have now seen in great detail how changes can affect the cash flow of a firm and how, as part of the planning process, this can help the business make financial decisions. You can see how a proposition for loan or overdraft facilities can be assessed using the forecast to see its effect and isolate its weakest points, so that they can be protected as far as possible.

Self-assessment questions

1. What are budgets?

2. What are cash flow forecasts and who would be interested in them?

3. Why is cash and profit different?

4. Why is depreciation not included in the cash flow forecast?

5. Why is it important to reflect the timings of cash received and paid?

6. How does the giving and taking of credit affect cash flow?

7. How can a cash budget be used in monitoring the success of a business in meeting repayments of overdrafts and loans?

8. What would you expect to see in a cash budget for a seasonal business, such as a firework manufacturer?

9. Distinguishing between capital and revenue expenditure is important when drawing up a trading, profit and loss account and balance sheet. Is this relevant when preparing a cash budget?

10. Name two cash inflows you would expect to see in a cash budget.

Unit 13

Concepts and Conventions of Accounting

Objectives

At the end of this Unit you will be able to:
- describe the impact of SSAP 2
- describe the requirements of SSAP 9
- describe the requirements of SSAP 12
- describe the requirements of SSAP 22
- describe the requirements of FRS 1
- describe the requirements of FRS 3.

1 Introduction

1.1 In this Unit we will look at several accounting standards that need to be followed in preparing financial accounts for larger organisations. If you look at the published accounts of Stock Exchange quoted companies, you will see their use explained and applied. Statements of Standard Accounting Practice (SSAP) and Financial Reporting Standards (FRS) are both forms of accounting standards.

1.2 You do not need a detailed knowledge of the SSAPs and FRSs that we look at in this Unit but you do need to understand what they cover. In this Unit we will outline SSAPs 2, 9, 12 and 22, and FRSs 1 and 3.

2 SSAP 2 disclosure of accounting policies

2.1 There are a number of SSAPs which set down basic rules for the production of the accounts. Different accountants might interpret the same basic information differently and therefore produce different answers.

2.2 SSAP 2 requires the business to disclose why it is exempt from the four fundamental concepts, which will be detailed, and the accounting policies adopted for any items deemed material or critical.

2.3 The four fundamental concepts are:

(i) **Going concern concept**. It is assumed that a business is a going concern and it will continue in business. If it is soon to close, a statement of affairs may be used instead of a balance sheet. The values could be quite different from the book value as they are to be sold and new liabilities created in respect of, say, redundancy payments.

(ii) **Accruals concept**. Unless otherwise stated, it is assumed that revenues and expenses have been received and incurred and the date of payment not reached.

(iii) **Consistency concept**. The accounting policy used for, say, valuing assets, remains the same each year. If a change is required, say, in the depreciation method, then this must be disclosed, along with its effect on the profit.

(iv) **Prudence concept**. This is to prevent the anticipation of profits. It requires companies to provide for likely losses.

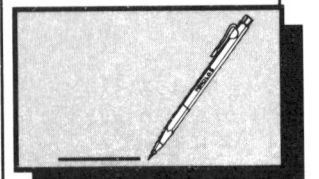

Student Activity 1

Give examples of the application of the accruals and prudence concepts from the topics you have already studied earlier in this course.

Feedback

2.4 You probably realised that accruals and prepayments arise from the accruals concept. And accounting for bad and doubtful debts are examples of applying prudence.

2.5 Other areas covered by SSAP 2 are outlined below.

Accounting bases

2.6 There are different bases for valuing assets and liabilities. They are different but equally acceptable, as you have already seen.

Accounting policies

2.7 Examples of accounting policies are:

(a) depreciation

(b) stock and work-in-progress

(c) research and development

(d) deferred taxation

(e) long-term contracts

(f) repairs and renewals

(g) hire purchase

(h) leasing

(i) goodwill

(j) property development.

2.8 These are some items to give you an idea; indeed all the common ones are included. These are the bases adopted by the companies which for they are most suitable. The disclosure of the particular bases used for some of the above items allows anyone looking at the accounts to know how the assets and liabilities have been valued.

3 SSAP 9 Stocks and work-in-progress

3.1 Stocks often represent a material amount in the business's balance sheet. Over or under-valuation resulting in distortions occurring in reported profit levels and net total assets, while taxation may be under or over-paid. In addition, an error in one year's stock figures will have a knock-on effect in the results of the next year.

Student Activity 2

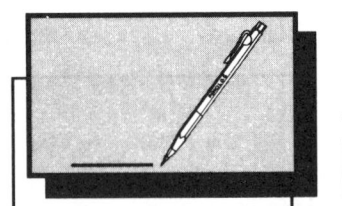

Explain why there should be a knock-on effect from one year to the next.

Feedback

3.2 There is a knock-on effect because the closing stock of one year is the opening stock of the next and both opening and closing stocks appear in the trading account. There is, therefore, a direct impact on the results from errors in stock figures.

3.3 Limited companies must appoint a qualified auditor whose job is to report that the accounts show a true and fair view. The auditor will check that the business has complied with SSAP 9. Therefore this is an important SSAP.

3.4 This SSAP states that the normal basis of stock valuation is the lower of cost and net realisable value.

3.5 **Cost** is identified by SSAP 9 as being expenditure which has been incurred in the normal course of business in bringing the product or service to its present location and condition.

3.6 A manufacturer may therefore calculate his stock in the following way:

Raw materials	500
Wages of production workers	1,000
	1,500

3.7 Note that the manufacturer has added together those costs involved in the items manufactured, which is known as the *marginal cost basis*.

3.8 Alternatively, a manufacturer may add to this an amount in respect of overheads incurred in the manufacture of items – e.g. factory rent and heat. This is known as total cost basis.

3.9 **Net realisable value** means the estimated selling price less any further costs to be incurred, on completion of a product, e.g. advertising selling and delivery costs.

3.10 If an item of stock cost 4,000 but could only realise 3,000 then it should be valued at the lower figure of 3,000.

4 SSAP 12 Depreciation

4.1 SSAP 12 defines depreciation as the measure of the wearing out, consumption or other reduction in useful life of a fixed asset, whether through use, effluxion of time or obsolescence through technological changes.

4.2 More simply, this means that depreciation is the amount that an asset has reduced during the period of use by the firm.

4.3 Depreciation should be allocated so as to charge a fair proportion of cost or valuation to each accounting period expected to benefit from the use of an asset. Note that depreciation is referred to as amortisation in the case of leasehold properties.

4.4 The amount to be allocated to accounting periods depends on three factors.

Student Activity 3

You should be able to remember the three factors on which the amount to be allocated depends, from your earlier work. Write them down below.

Feedback

4.5 The factors are:

1 the cost of valuation on the asset

2 the expected useful life

3 the estimated residual value.

4.6 The disclosure requirements for depreciation of fixed assets are:

1 the depreciation method used

2 the useful economic life

3 the total depreciation for year

4 the gross amount of depreciable assets and the related, accumulated depreciation.

5 SSAP 22 Goodwill

5.1 Goodwill is the difference between the fair value of a business as a whole and the aggregate of the fair values of its separable net assets.

5.2 **Fair value** is the amount that an asset (or liability) can be identified and sold for without disposing of the business as a whole.

5.3 **Purchased goodwill** arising on the purchase of a business, the purchase price paid is over and above the cost of the net assets.

5.4 **Non-purchased goodwill** can arise when a going concern is worth more than the fair values of its net assets.

Treatment of Goodwill

5.5 Immediate write-off against reserves.

5.6 Amortise over its useful life (treat like depreciation). Useful life is decided when the goodwill comes into the business.

5.7 Goodwill should be disclosed in the accounts.

6 FRS 1 Cash flow Statements

6.1 FRS 1 was introduced after a number of apparently solvent companies had collapsed due to a lack of liquidity. One company that received a lot of publicity over this was the Polly Peck group. Consequently a revision in cash flow statements was brought into effect with the launch of FRS 1.

6.2 FRS 1 has the standard layout, which companies must follow. The objective of the statement is for companies to show how they generated their money and what they spent it on. The statement has several standard headings (see Unit 9).

6.3 The cash flow statement provides an indication of the financial policy adopted by the company and its effects on the company's financial position. Analysis will reveal how the company finances their long-term investments.

6.4 The cash flow statements can highlight potential over-trading activities where companies are trying to expand too quickly. Over-trading can result in:

- an increase in fixed assets
- An increase in stock
- reduction in credit given to debtors
- reduction in the bank balance
- increase in the credit taken from suppliers.

7 FRS 3 Reporting Financial Performance

7.1 The standard states its objective as being to aid users in understanding the performance achieved by a reporting entity in a period and to assist them in forming a basis for their assessment of future results and cash flows.

7.2 The key definitions are:

- **Ordinary activities** – any activities undertaken by the reporting entity that are in the normal course of their business. Ordinary activities include the effects on the reporting entity of any event in the various environments in which it operates, including the political, regulatory, economic and geographical environments, irrespective of the frequency or unusual nature of the events.

- **Extraordinary items** – material items possessing a high degree of abnormality which arise from events of transactions that fall outside the normal activities of the business. These items are extremely rare. These items should be shown separately on the face of the profit and loss account.

- **Exceptional items** – material items that derive from the normal activities of the business and need to be disclosed in the accounts to give a true and fair view. These should be disclosed separately by way of a note in the final accounts.

- **Prior year adjustments** – material adjustments applicable to prior periods arising from changes in accounting policies or from the correction of a fundamental error. Depending on the type of prior year adjustment, restate amounts for prior period and adjust opening balance of retained profit.

Student Activity 4

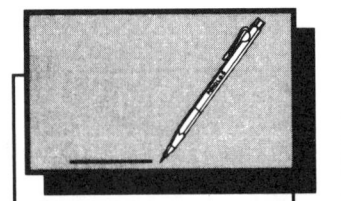

Which of the fundamental accounting concepts in SSAP 2 is broken through making a change in accounting policies?

Feedback

7.3　Consistency is the concept which is not being followed. This is acceptable if the result is that the change produces a 'true and fair view' of the profit and asset values of a business.

7.4　The format now used for the profit and loss account, incorporating the adjustments in FRS 3 is as follows:

Continuing operations	Discontinued operations
Normal operations	Normal operations
Item 1 as stated below	Item 1 stated below

Extraordinary items

7.5　(Item 1 refers to profits or losses on the sale or termination of an operation, costs of fundamental reorganisation or restructuring and profits or losses on the disposal of fixed assets.)

8　Summary

8.1　In this Unit you looked at various accounting standards. You saw that SSAP 2: Disclosure of accounting policies identifies the fundamental accounting concepts which underlie all accounting as well as accounting bases, such as straight-line depreciation, and accounting policies.

8.2　We then went on to look at SSAP 9: Stocks and work-in-progress, which gives guidance on stock valuation, and SSAP 12: Accounting for depreciation, which identifies the factors you need to think about when depreciating fixed assets, together with the disclosure requirements.

8.3 In addition we looked as SSAP 22: Accounting for goodwill which differentiates between purchased and non-purchased goodwill and identifies the optional approaches that may be used in dealing with purchased goodwill in the account: amortisation through the profit and loss account or immediate write-off against reserves.

8.4 Once again we looked briefly at FRS 1: Cash flow statements, which you looked at in depth earlier, before ending by looking at FRS 3: Reporting financial performance which identifies different forms of items in accounting deriving from ordinary, exceptional or extraordinary activities. Extraordinary activities are considered to be so rare that no examples are given in FRS 3 and none has been identified so far in practice.

Self-assessment questions

1. What are the fundamental accounting concepts identified in SSAP 2?

2. What else is covered in SSAP 2 other than the fundamental accounting concepts?

3. State the basic rule of stock valuation contained in SSAP 9.

4. Define 'net realisable value'.

5. State the matters which need to be disclosed in respect of the depreciation of fixed assets under SSAP 12.

6. Distinguish between purchased and non-purchased goodwill.

7. What are the optional treatments of goodwill contained in SSAP 22?

8. What is the objective of FRS 1?

9. What is the objective of FRS 3?

10. Define ordinary activities in accordance with FRS 3.

Unit 14

Bank Reconciliation

> **Objectives**
>
> At the end of this Unit you will be able to:
> - draw up a reconciliation of the bank account to the cash book.

1 Introduction

1.1 In this Unit we will look at the reconciliation of the bank account to the cash book. This is a regular task in business because business records need to be monitored against those of the bank to ensure that no errors occur and no direct debits, etc. are overlooked. You saw when we looked at incomplete records that this is an important task to determine the bank figure which should appear in the end of year balance sheet, too, as the bank account balance on any one day is likely to differ from the business expectation of the bank balance because cheques have not been presented, for example.

2 The reconciliation of the bank account to the cash book

2.1 Bank reconciliations are carried out in most organisations whenever a bank statement is received. This ensures that any errors or problems are picked up as early as possible.

2.2 The bank reconciliation statement is drawn up by comparing the items in the cash book with the bank statement. Where they agree they are crossed off.

2.3 The reconciliation statement starts with the closing bank account statement, then cheques not presented are deducted from the balance and credit items not yet presented are added.

2.4 The new balance should then equal the balance in the cash book.

Student Activity 1

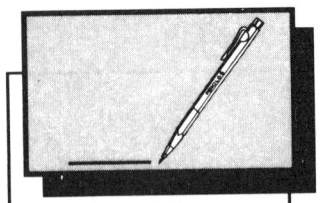

How might differences arise between an organisations records and the bank statement?

Feedback

2.5 Differences arise because of the following:

(i) Cheques issued are included in the cash book but have not yet been presented and therefore do not appear in the bank statement.

(ii) Credit items paid in are in the cash book but have not yet appeared on the statement. This, as with (i), can be due to the fact that at the date the statement was produced it did not include these items but they will appear on the next statement. Remember that several cheques received and entered into the cash book individually may be bulked together on a credit.

(iii) Payments may be on the statement but not in the cash book, such as bank interest, charges and standing orders or direct debits.

(iv) Payments may have been made directly into the bank account by a third party, such as for a refund. These will not appear in the cash book and their existence will only be realised when the bank statement is received.

2.6 The relevant items must be added or subtracted from the closing bank balance to agree with the closing balance in the cash book. When the reconciliation is completed any items (iii) and (iv) will need to be entered into the cash book so that the records are kept up to date. Its just like balancing your own bank statement.

Student Activity 2

Prepare a bank reconciliation by comparing the following cash book against the bank statement.

Cash book

	£		£
Balance b/d	1,000	Cheque 001	100
Paid in	250	Cheque 002	50
Paid in	150	Cheque 003	75
Paid in	60	Cheque 004	200
		Cheque 005	300
		Balance c/d	735
	1,460		1,460

Bank statement

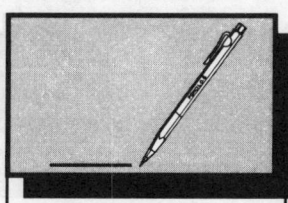

	Dr	Cr	Balance
	£	£	£
Balance			1,000 Cr
Cheque 001	100		900 Cr
Cheque 003	75		825 Cr
Cash/Cheques		250	1,075 Cr
Cheque 005	300		775 Cr
Cash/Cheques		150	925 Cr

Feedback

2.7 Your bank reconciliation should agree with this:

Bank Reconciliation Statement as at [date]

		£	
Balance per bank statement		925	Cr
Add banking not yet credited		60	
		985	Cr
Less cheques not yet presented for payment			
002	50		
004	200	250	
Balance per cash book		735	Cr

Student Activity 3

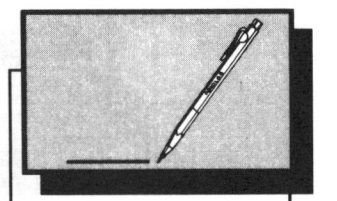

Explain what the above bank reconciliation shows.

Feedback

2.8 You probably thought this through as you drew up the reconciliation statement. It is always important to fully understand what you are doing so that you get the direction of the adjustments correct. Writing down an explanation should have highlighted the important features for you.

2.9 The bank reconciliation shows that the bank statement balance has a higher balance than the business expected. Investigation shows that two cheques have yet to be presented. In addition, 60 which has been paid in, perhaps in the nightsafe or at a different branch, has yet to be credited to the bank account.

2.10 In some cases you will be required to update the cash book first. To do this you need to identify items that are entered on the bank statement that belong to the company for example, direct credits, interest, bank charges etc. Try this for yourself.

Student Activity 4

Cash book

	£		£
Balance b/d	5,000	Cheque 001	200
Paid in	300	Cheque 002	400
Paid in	500	Cheque 003	300
		Balance c/d	4,900
	5,800		5,800

Bank statement

	Dr £	Cr £	Balance £	
Balance			5,000	Cr
Cheque 001	200		4,800	Cr
Cash/Cheques		300	5,100	Cr
Cheque 002	400		4,700	Cr
Bank charges	50		4,650	Cr
Cash/Cheques		500	5,150	Cr
VAT refund		200	5,350	Cr

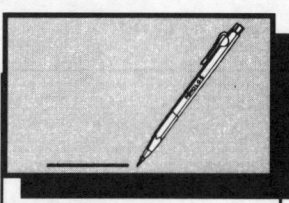

Feedback

2.11 Your updated cash book should look like this:

Updated cash book

Balance b/f	4,900	Bank charges	50
VAT refund	200	Balance c/f	5,050
	5,100		5,100
Balance b/f	5,050		

Bank reconciliation statement as at [date]

Balance as per cash book	5,050
Add cheque 003 not yet presented	300
Balance as per bank statement	5,350

2.12 Remember, for credit balances the bank account is a debit item in the firm's cash book because it is an asset. In the bank's book it is shown as a credit balance because it is a liability and will at some time have to be paid back to the customer.

2.13 When the bank account is overdrawn the complete opposite is true. So any outstanding cheques must be added to the overdrawn balance to present the true picture of indebtedness to the bank. Try the earlier exercises but reverse the position and make the bank balance overdrawn to make sure you can deal with this situation.

3 Summary

3.1 You now know, if you didn't before, how to reconcile the cash book to the bank statement, and you have had some practice. Sometimes you will only need to draw up a bank reconciliation statement. However, if items have been entered into the bank account before the business is aware of them, an adjustment will need to be made to the cash book. Typical examples would be bank charges and interest.

3.2 Remember, it's just like reconciling your own bank statement to your cheque book, so you can practice this every month!

Self-assessment questions

1. Why are bank reconciliation statements drawn up?

2. When are bank reconciliation statements likely to be drawn up?

3. What would you expect to see as the first and last items in a bank reconciliation statement?

4. How is a bank reconciliation statement headed up?

5. Why will there be differences between the cash book and the bank statement?

6. Give two items that may appear on the bank statement but may not be entered in the cash book.

7. Give two items that may appear in the cash book but not be on the bank statement.

8. On what side of the cash book will bank charges appear?

9. Is a bank overdraft a liability or an asset in the books of the business?

10. Why is a bank reconciliation useful when preparing final accounts from incomplete records?

Unit 15

Ratio Analysis

> **Objectives**
>
> At the end of this Unit you will be able to:
> - identify and use some common accounting ratios
> - explain their limitations.

1 Introduction

1.1 Ratio analysis is a method of analysing a company's performance over a period of time and can be extremely useful to the management of a company and to bank managers when faced with requests for loans.

1.2 Ratios fall into two broad categories: profitability and liquidity.

1.3 We will also take a look at the limitations of ratios. It is important to be aware of these to ensure they are used properly.

1.4 First we will look at profitability ratios.

2 Gross profit ratio

$$\frac{\text{Gross profit}}{\text{Sales}} \times 100$$

2.1 This measures the gross profit as a percentage of sales and indicates how effectively the company has controlled the cost of goods sold. An increase in gross profit percentage might be due to the company's ability to raise the selling price without a corresponding increase in the cost of goods sold. A decrease in gross profit percentage might be due to a reduction in selling price against stable costs.

3 Net profit ratio

$$\frac{\text{Net profit}}{\text{Sales}} \times 100$$

3.1 This measures the net profit as a percentage of sales and indicates how effectively the company has controlled all their costs. A decrease in net profit percentage is usually due to an increase in expenses.

4 Return on capital employed

$$\frac{\text{Net profit before tax and interest}}{\text{Capital employed*}}$$

* If sole trader, use closing capital figure.
If company, use total of shares and reserves.

4.1 Return on capital employed (ROCE) measures the return on the long-term funds employed in the business and is an indication of whether a company has successfully utilised its assets during the period.

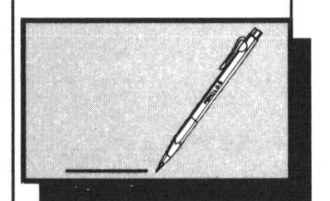

Student Activity 1

From the information below, calculate the net profit ratio, gross profit ratio and return on capital employed:

Sales for year	100,000
Cost of sales	50,000
Expenses	40,000
Dividends paid and proposed	5,000
Capital employed	40,000

Ignore tax and interest in your calculations.

Feedback

4.2 Before you can calculate the ratios, you need to determine the figures for gross and net profit. These are as follows:

Gross profit = Sales − Cost of sales = 100,000 − 50,000 = 50,000
Net profit = Gross profit − Expenses = 50,000 − 40,000 = 10,000

4.3 Dividends are, of course, an appropriation and do not feature in the calculations.

4.5 The ratios, therefore, are:

Gross profit ratio = $\dfrac{50,000 \times 100}{100,000}$ = 50%

Net profit ratio = $\dfrac{10,000 \times 100}{100,000}$ = 10%

Return on capital employed = $\dfrac{10,000 \times 100}{40,000}$ = 40%

4.5 Well now turn to liquidity ratios. These ratios measure the company's ability to pay their short-term debts.

5 Working capital ratio

$$\dfrac{\text{Current assets}}{\text{Current liabilities}}$$

5.1 This, as we have already discussed, relates to short-term liquidity. The correct working capital ratio will depend on the type of business, but as a general rule many textbooks quote 2:1, so if current assets are 4,000 and current liabilities are 2,000 the working capital ratio would be:

$\dfrac{4,000}{2,000}$ 2:1

5.2 The current assets cover the current liabilities twice.

6 Liquidity or quick ratio

6.1 The liquidity or quick ratio refers only to items which can quickly be transferred into cash, and so for this reason stock is left out unless sales are on a cash basis.

$\dfrac{\text{Liquid assets}}{\text{Current liabilities}}$:1

6.2 Taking the earlier example, if stock were 2,000 the ratio would be:

$$\frac{2,000}{2,000} = 1:1$$

6.3 A ratio of 1:1 is considered acceptable. Below this there would not be sufficient liquid funds to meet the commitments. It must, however, be borne in mind that all the current liabilities are included, some of which, like tax, may not be payable for some time. This ratio is also sometimes referred to as the acid test of solvency.

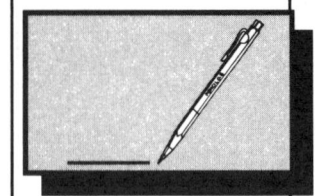

Student Activity 2

From the information below, calculate the working capital ratio, and liquidity ratio:

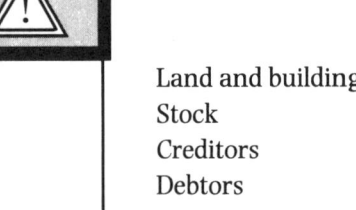

	£
Land and buildings	30,000
Stock	11,000
Creditors	8,000
Debtors	10,000
Long-term mortgage loan	20,000
Cash	1,000
Bank overdraft	3,000

Feedback

6.4   Again you need to make some calculations before you can calculate the ratios. You must decide which of the items are current assets and which are current liabilities. Then you can total the current assets and liabilities.

6.5   Current assets are stock, debtors and cash, totalling 22,000.

6.6   Current liabilities comprise creditors and bank overdraft, totalling 11,000.

6.7   Therefore the working capital ratio = 22,000 : 11,000 = 2 : 1.

6.8   The liquidity ratio = 22,000 – 11,000 : 11,000 = 1 : 1.

6.9   We'll now look at further measures of liquidity.

7   Rate of stock turnover

$$\frac{\text{Cost of goods sold}}{\text{Average stock level}}$$

7.1   This is a measurement of how quickly the stock is turning over. There may be stock which is hard to sell, because it has gone out of fashion or style etc. and where there is a considerable increase in stock levels this must be considered. By using the ratio you can find out. This ratio can also expressed in days:

$$\frac{\text{Average stock}}{\text{Cost of goods sold}} \times 365$$

8   Collection time of debtors and creditors

$$\text{Debtors} = \frac{\text{Average debtors}}{\text{Credit sales}} \times 365$$

$$\text{Creditors} = \frac{\text{Average creditors}}{\text{Credit purchases}} \times 365$$

8.1   These figures show how long it is taking to collect and repay the debts. If there is a significant change in the debtors, then the firm may be pressing for quicker payment because it has liquidity problems, or longer to pay in that there could be some bad debts. If creditors are being paid quicker is there pressure from the supplier for payment?

8.2   Another important area to look at is capital adequacy, or gearing.

9 Gearing

$$\frac{\text{Long-term liabilities + Preference shares} \times 100}{\text{Equity*}}$$

*Shareholders' funds

9.1 This examines the extent to which the company relies on borrowed funds and will be faced with high interest charges and may find it difficult to raise further finance.

10 Interest cover

$$\frac{\text{Interest}}{\text{Net profit}} = \text{No. of times}$$

10.1 This indicates the number of times the interest can be covered by the net profit. The higher, the better.

10.2 Now put what you have learnt together by working through the following example.

10.3 The balance sheets and revenue accounts for the year ended 30 June of G.E. TUP and D. OWN are given below.

Balance sheets as at 30 June

	G.E. TUP		D. OWN	
	£		£	
Fixed assets at cost	60,000		30,000	
Less provision for depreciation	20,000	40,000	10,000	20,000
Current assets				
Stocks	57,000		30,000	
Debtors	22,000		20,000	
Cash	11,000		10,000	
	90,000		60,000	
Less current liabilities	30,000	60,000	30,000	30,000
Net assets employed		100,000		50,000
Proprietors' capital		100,000		50,000
		100,000		50,000

Revenue accounts for the year ended 30 June

	G.E. TUP		D. OWN	
	£		£	
Sales		160,000		120,000
Less cost of goods sold				
Opening stock	39,000		20,000	
Purchases	114,000		85,000	
	153,000		105,000	
Less closing stock	57,000	96,000	30,000	75,000
Gross profit		64,000		45,000
Less expenses		56,000		39,000
Net profit		8,000		6,000

10.3 It can be assumed that stocks have increased evenly throughout the year and that both businesses are in the same trade.

Required:

Calculate the following ratios for each business:

(i) Return on the capital employed

(ii) Gross profit percentage

(iii) Net profit percentage

(iv) Current ratio

(v) Liquid ratio

(vi) Stock turnover

(vii) Debtors collection period.

10.4 Work through these calculations.

				TUP	OWN
(i)	ROCE	Net profit / Capital	x 100	8,000 x 100 / 100,000 = 8%	6,000 x 100 / 50,000 = 12%
(ii)	GP %	Gross profit / Sales	x 100	64,000 x 100 / 160,000 = 40%	45,000 x 100 / 120,000 = 37.5%
(iii)	NP%	Net profit / Sales	x 100	8,000 x 100 / 160,000 = 5%	6,000 x 100 / 120,000 = 5%
(iv)	Current ratio	Current Assets / Current liabilities		90,000 / 30,000 = 3:1	60,000 / 30,000 = 2:1
(v)	Liquid	Current assets – Stock / Current liabilities		90,000 – 57,000 / 30,000 = 1.1:1	60,000 – 30,000 / 30,000 = 1:1
(vi)	Stock turnover	Cost of goods sold / Average stock		96,000 / (39,000 + 57,000)/2 = 2 times	75,000 / (20,000 + 30,000)/2 = 3 times
(vii)	Debtors turnover	Debtors x 365 / Sales		22,000 x 365 / 160,000 = 50 days	20,000 x 365 / 120,000 = 61 days

10.5 Calculating ratios is just part of interpretation. What is more important is that you can use the ratios to understand what has happened in a business over time or be able to compare businesses.

Student Activity 3

From the ratios in the example above, compare the liquidity and profitability of TUP and OWN.

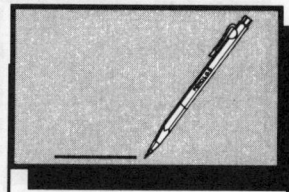

Feedback

10.6 The ratios provide limited information but some general conclusions can be drawn.

10.7 OWN produces a higher return on the owner's investment or capital employed and because both businesses have a net profit ratio of 5%, this indicates that OWN is making a more effective use of its resources. As TUP has a better gross profit ratio, this probably indicates that the administration of OWN is much more effective and TUP should look at this area.

10.8 Moving on to liquidity, TUP has a higher working capital and turns over stock more slowly than OWN. This area may need attention and could improve profitability. TUP appears to offer less credit to customers. This may be a policy of the businesses or indicate less successful credit control by OWN.

10.9 Clearly to analyse this information further, you would need to ask questions of the owners of the business. This would be the approach you could take when lending money to businesses.

10.10 You have now calculated ratios and analysed what those ratios mean to some extent. Now attempt the following comprehensive exercise which brings all these points together. Draw up your answer on separate paper.

Student Activity 4

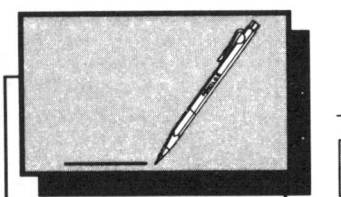

Turners Ltd trading profit and loss accounts

	Year 1 (£000)	Year 2 (£000)	Year 3 (£000)
Turnover	300	360	450
Cost of sales	240	288	375
Gross profit	60	72	75
Expenses	45	57	57
Pre-tax profit	15	15	18
Tax	6	6	6
Retained profit	9	9	12
Profit and loss b/fwd	30	39	48
Profit and loss c/fwd	39	48	60

Balance sheets

	Year 1 (£000)	Year 2 (£000)	Year 3 (£000)
Fixed assets	600	606	597
Current assets			
Stock	30	24	30
Debtors	45	39	48
Cash	–	9	15
	75	72	93
Current liabilities			
Creditors	48	48	48
Bank	6	–	–
	54	48	48
Net current assets	21	24	45
Net assets employed	621	630	642
Financed by			
Ordinary shares	582	582	582
Reserves	39	48	60
	621	630	642

Use as many ratios as you can to asses the liquidity and profitability position of Turners Ltd. Comment on your results.

Feedback

10.11 Check your ratio calculations with these:

		Year 1	Year 2	Year 3
Liquidity current ratio	$\dfrac{\text{Current assets}}{\text{Current liabilities}}$	$\dfrac{75}{54}$ = 1.39:1	$\dfrac{72}{48}$ = 1.5:1	$\dfrac{93}{48}$ = 1.94:1
Liquid ratio	$\dfrac{\text{Current assets} - \text{Stock}}{\text{Current liabilities}}$	$\dfrac{45}{54}$ = .83:1	$\dfrac{48}{48}$ = 1:1	$\dfrac{63}{48}$ = 1.31:1
Stock turn	$\dfrac{\text{Cost of goods sold}}{\text{Average stock}}$	N/A N/A	$\dfrac{288}{(30+24)/2}$ = 10.7 times	$\dfrac{375}{(24+30)/2}$ = 13.9 times
Debtor collection	$\dfrac{\text{Debtors} \times 365}{\text{Sales}}$	$\dfrac{45 \times 365}{300}$ = 55 days	$\dfrac{39 \times 365}{360}$ = 40 days	$\dfrac{48 \times 365}{450}$ = 39 days
Profitability ROCE	$\dfrac{\text{Net profit} \times 100}{\text{Capital}}$	$\dfrac{15 \times 100}{621}$ = 2.4%	$\dfrac{15 \times 100}{630}$ = 2.4%	$\dfrac{18 \times 100}{642}$ = 2.8%
	$\dfrac{\text{Gross profit} \times 100}{\text{Sales}}$	$\dfrac{60 \times 100}{300}$ = 20%	$\dfrac{72 \times 100}{360}$ = 20%	$\dfrac{75 \times 100}{450}$ = 16.7%
	$\dfrac{\text{Net profit} \times 100}{\text{Sales}}$	$\dfrac{15 \times 100}{300}$ = 5%	$\dfrac{15 \times 100}{360}$ = 4.2%	$\dfrac{18 \times 100}{450}$ = 4%

10.12 Liquidity. The liquidity position of Turners has improved from 1.39 to 1.94. This means that they are able to meet their short-term debts as they fall due. This is a good position for the company to be in. The stock turn period has improved from 10 times to 13 times per year, which means that their stock is moving quicker; also, Turners are collecting their debts quicker, which means they are able to improve their current ratio and cash flow.

10.13 Profitability. The return on capital employed has improved steadily over the three-year period. However, both the net profit and gross profit percentages have dropped, which probably means that their cost of sales and expenses have increased but these increases have not been passed on to their customers.

11 The limitations of ratios

11.1 The accounts must be compared with those of previous years to establish a trend. When using the ratios you must bear in mind the kind of business you are dealing with, as there will be different effects on different kinds of accounts.

11.2 Ratios should make you question; they do not provide explanations, so you may need more information. They should not be used in isolation. One poor ratio does not necessarily mean problems; another may answer the question.

11.3 Remember inflation and its effect on the accounts: this will be reflected in the ratios. Businesses use different policies for valuing stock (FIFO, LIFO, etc. see Unit 16). If you are comparing similar companies this must be considered.

11.4 Another limitation of ratios is that they don't take account of seasonal business, so you must do so. A fireworks factory will probably have high stocks running up to 5 November. The shops may not start taking the goods until October, so this high stock value is reasonable.

12 Summary

12.1 Ratios can be a useful tool to interpret the accounts, but they must be used with some thought and consideration for what is behind the figures and not taken on face value. The more practice you have in working out and interpreting what might be happening, the easier it will become.

12.2 In this Unit you looked at commonly used ratios for profitability, liquidity and capital adequacy.

Self-assessment questions

1. Identify two profitability ratios other than return on capital employed.

2. Give the formula for calculating return on capital employed.

3. What is the formula for the working capital ratio?

4. What is the difference between the working capital ratio and the liquidity ratio?

5. How is the speed at which customers who are provided with goods on credit pay-up measured?

6. What does the rate of stock turnover measure?

7. Give the formula for gearing.

8. Why is the ratio of interest cover important to a lending banker?

9. Give two limitations of ratio analysis.

10. Why are ratios used?

16

Unit 16

Valuation of Stock, Work-in-Progress and Manufacturing Accounts

Objectives

At the end of this Unit you will be able to:
- calculate the value of stock and of work-in-progress
- prepare a manufacturing account.

1 Introduction

1.1 In this Unit we will look further at stock and its role in accounting. So far you have seen how stock is valued and how it is dealt with in the trading account and balance sheet.

1.2 However, we have yet to look at manufacturing businesses. In these, raw materials and work-in-progress also need to be considered and these are brought into a manufacturing account. We shall consider manufacturing accounts and stock in this Unit, beginning with a revision of stock valuation.

2 Why is the valuation of stock important?

2.1 As you already know, the stock figure is used to calculate the gross profit, which in turn gives you the net profit and the closing stock figure as it appears on the balance sheet. If, therefore, some stock was over-valued, the profit earned would be unrealistic and vice versa. As well as this, another valuation we have to consider is the debtors figure, in that the outstanding balances reflect the value of the goods bought. The firm must therefore decide how the goods sold, and those that remain, are allocated a cost and therefore a valuation.

Student Activity 1

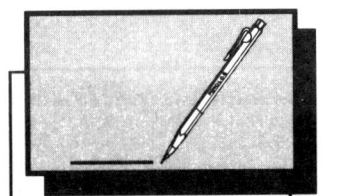

Think about SSAP 9: Stock and work-in-progress. What is the rule for valuing stock?

Feedback

2.2 The normal valuation undertaken by firms is cost or net realisable value, whichever is lower.

3 Cost

3.1 This covers all the associated costs of bringing the goods to their present state. So, if finished goods are bought for resale, it is all the costs associated with this including the overheads. If it is the production of some goods, cost includes all associated costs including direct labour (to produce the goods) and other overheads.

4 Net realisable value

4.1 This is the selling price less any other costs (such as advertising and marketing).

4.2 So if goods cost 200 and sell for 500, and there is a 10% commission on the sale price for the selling agent, the net realisable value is:

	£
Sale price	500
Commission	50
Net realisable value	450

4.3 Net realisable value is of particular importance when the cost of the goods/parts is rising, if the selling price of the completed goods is falling, if the goods have deteriorated or gone out of fashion or use, or if there were some errors in either the production or selling costs.

4.4 The calculated lowest figure derived through either cost or net realisable value is therefore the price to be used to value the goods. To do this, though, you need to know what you paid for the goods and the likely selling price.

5 Method of assessing the stock

5.1 There are three main methods:

- FIFO
- LIFO
- weighted average cost (AVCO).

FIFO

5.2 This means first in first out. So the goods in stock that were bought first are deemed to be sold first. In assessing the profit on the transaction, the cost that the first goods were bought at is the starting point. When all these goods have been sold you move on to the next batch, which may be at a higher price.

LIFO

5.3 This means last in first out. Here, the latest goods bought (and probably at the highest price) are deemed to be sold first and the older and cheaper stock sold only when the latest batch has been sold.

5.4 You will probably already have realised that these two methods of assessment will present a different valuation of the same stock.

Student Activity 2

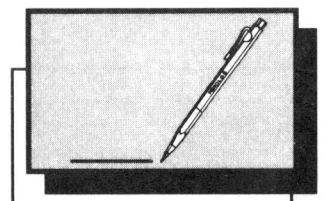

Using the two methods calculate the value of the stock left, excluding any associated costs.

Units bought   Units sold

1 Jan   200 @ 10
1 Feb   200 @ 15   31 Jan   100
1 Mar   200 @ 20   1 Apr   400

Feedback

5.5 Your calculations should agree with these:

FIFO

Units sold		Units remaining
31 Jan	100 @ £10	100 @ £10
1 Apr	100 @ £10	= £1,000
	200 @ £15	
	100 @ £20	
		100 @ £20
		= £2,000

LIFO

Units sold		Units remaining
31 Jan	100 @ £10	100 @ £10
		= £1,000
1 Apr	200 @ £20	100 @ £10
	200 @ £15	= £1,000

5.6 By employing these two different methods of using up the stock we have a difference of 1,000. This is because with FIFO the most expensive stock is deemed to be remaining, thus achieving a higher value. The estimation of the cost of goods sold is higher using LIFO because the cost of buying the goods is closer to the sale price being the stock most recently acquired.

5.7 **Note**: This assumes, as is invariably the case, that prices are rising.

Weighted average cost (AVCO)

5.8 Under this method a calculation is made when goods are bought and an average is taken of the first batch's cost and the new purchase. This price is then held until the next batch of goods is bought. So the cost of these goods is averaged out. For example:

100 units @ 10	= 1,000	
100 units @ 18	= 1,800	$\frac{2,800}{200} = 14$
200	2,800	

Units issued at 14.

Student Activity 3

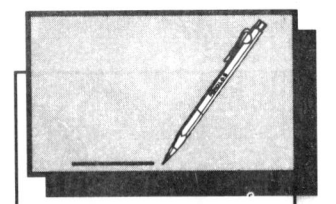

From the information given in Activity 2, calculate the value of the remaining stock using the weighted average cost method.

Feedback

5.9 Check your calculations against these:

Average Cost

1	Jan	Bought	200 @ £10	= 2,000	200	= 10*
31	Jan	Sold balances	100 @ £10	= 1,000 1,000		
1	Feb	Bought balances	200 @ £15 200	= 3,000 4,000	300	= £13.33
1	March	Bought balances	200 @ £20 500	= 4,000 8,000	500	= 16.00*
1	April	Sold balances	400 @ £16* 100	= 6,400 1,600		

5.10 * As its name suggests average cost will usually result in a final balance between LIFO and FIFO in a period of constantly falling or rising prices, but this is not an invariable rule.

6 Work-in-progress

6.1 Stock not only includes goods for resale but also raw material, finished goods and work-in-progress (WIP).

6.2 Work-in-progress is, as it sounds, work on producing some goods or equipment which is not yet completed to the stage where these are ready for sale. Valuation of WIP is the cost including the overheads directly related to production. Some items (such as an oil rig) will take years to build, so only when, say, 25–30% of the work is completed can it be considered to be contributing any profit.

6.3 In prudent accounting only two-thirds of any expected profit to date is taken. From their previous experience firms with long-term projects will use prudent figures based on their own methods. These must, however, be realistic and they must state the basis on which the valuation has been made.

7 SSAP 9

7.1 The Statement of Standard Accounting Practice No. 9 covers the valuation of stock and work-in-progress. This accounting rule must be followed when the accounts are declared.

7.2 Accounts must state the basis of the valuation of stock and work-in-progress. The guidelines/rules we have discussed conform to SSAP 9 but, as you have probably realised already, there are many possibilities for the valuation; this statement narrows the avenues open and enforces prudent accounting.

8 Manufacturing accounts

8.1 So far in our accounting progress we have concentrated on businesses which buy-in finished goods. In a manufacturing concern, of course, it is necessary to look at the cost of making the goods before we can work on the trading profit and loss account.

8.2 The manufacturing account goes above the trading account and deals with all matters relating to the costs of manufacturing goods. These costs fall into two categories: prime (or direct) costs and production (or indirect) costs.

8.3 **Variable or direct costs** are those which can be attributed to the manufacturing process itself. The three main costs in this area are:

1. *Direct labour* – i.e. workers who are actually working at making something as opposed to those who may be supervising or servicing them. So, for example, someone working on the production line in a factory will be treated as a prime cost, whereas the foreman supervising the worker will be an indirect cost; the goods can be made even if the foreman is not there.

2. *Raw materials* – e.g. wood is bought in timber lengths and having gone through the manufacturing process comes out the other end as finished goods.

3. *Other direct costs* – again the main criterion is whether a cost can be attributed directly to the manufacturing process. For example, if a production line is powered by electricity which can be monitored separately from the supply to the rest of the factory and offices, this would be entered as a direct cost.

8.4 **Production or indirect costs** are those which are involved in the manufacturing area but cannot be directly related to the manufacturing process. Examples of indirect costs are heat, light and rates.

8.5 The main criterion to apply is if there were no production going on, would I still need to make payments for this? If the answer is no, it is direct, if yes it is indirect. For example, I must pay rates on my factory even when it is lying idle; indirect cost; but I do not have to pay for electricity to run my production line if there is no production; direct cost.

8.6 Work through the following example of a manufacturing account.

8.7 From the following balances construct a manufacturing account

	£
Raw materials	28,000
Carriage in of raw materials	500
Manufacturing wages	14,000
Light and heat	1,000
Rent and rates	1,250
Depreciation on machinery	750
Other factory wages	6,000
Opening stock of raw materials	4,000
Closing stock of raw materials	2,500

8.8 The manufacturing account is as follows:

Manufacturing account

Opening stock of raw materials	4,000
Add purchase of raw materials	28,000
	32,000
Add carriage in raw materials	500
	32,500
Less Closing stock of raw materials	2,500
Cost of raw materials consumed	30,000
Add manufacturing wages	14,000
Prime cost	44,000
Factory indirect costs	
Light and heat	1,000
Rent and rates	1,250
Depreciation	750
Other wages	6,000
Cost of production *	53,000

* This cost of production is transferred to the trading account.

Notes

8.9 There is no such thing as sales in a manufacturing account, therefore there is no profit on a manufacturing account. The cost is simply transferred to the profit and loss account and treated in the same way as purchases (there may, of course, be opening and closing stocks of finished goods in the normal way to take into account).

8.10 Work-in-progress is accounted for at the end of the manufacturing account; add work-in-progress at the beginning of the year and deduct work-in-progress at the end of the year.

8.11 Stocks of finished goods appear in the trading account.

8.12 Sometimes costs are to be divided between the manufacturing account and the profit and loss account.

8.13 Now work through the following complete example.

The following balances were among those extracted from the books of Bucket, a manufacturing business on 31 December 19X5.

	Dr	Cr
Sales		270,000
Production wages	50,000	
Purchase of raw materials	100,000	
Depreciation of manufacturing equipment in 19X5	10,000	
Production overhead	7,500	
Rent	9,000	
Depreciation of office equipment	2,000	
Salaries of sales staff	16,000	
Delivery costs	12,000	
Advertising costs	6,000	
General administration	22,000	
Stock at 1 January 19X5		
Raw materials	15,000	
WIP	1,500	
Finished goods	20,000	

Notes

1 Stock at 31 December 19X5

   Raw materials   12,500

   WIP   2,500

   Finished goods   27,000

2 Two-thirds of the rent relates to the factory.

The manufacturing, trading and profit and loss account follows.

Bucket
Manufacturing, trading profit and loss account
for the year ending 31 December 19X5

	£	£
O/S raw materials	15,000	
Purchase of raw materials	100,000	
	115,000	
Less closing stock of raw materials	12,500	
Cost of raw materials consumed	102,500	
Add production wages	50,000	
Prime cost	152,500	
Factory indirect costs		
Depreciation	10,000	
Expenses	7,500	
Rent (2/3 x 9,000)	6,000	
Total cost of production	176,000	
WIP 1 January 19X5	1,500	
WIP 31 December 19X5	(2,500)	
Cost of goods completed transferred to trading account	175,000	
Sales		270,000
O/S finished goods	20,000	
Add transferred from production	175,000	
	195,000	
Less closing stock of finished goods	27,000	
Cost of goods sold		168,000
Gross profit		102,000
Less expenses		
Rent (1/3 x 9,000)	3,000	
Depreciation of office equipment	2,000	
Sales staffs salaries	16,000	
Delivery costs	12,000	
Advertising	6,000	
General administration	22,000	
		61,000
Net profit		41,000

8.10 To check your understanding of manufacturing accounts, complete the following exercise. Prepare your accounts.

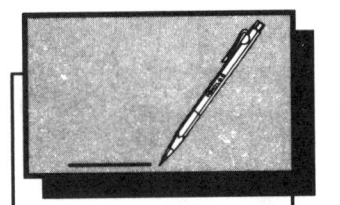

Student Activity 4

The following is the trial balance of Ambergate, a sole trader and manufacturer at 31 December 19X0.

	£000s	£000s
Sales		500
Capital		110
Purchase of raw materials	126	
Loan interest	12	
Manufacturing wages	73	
Manufacturing plant	164	
Accumulated depreciation on manufacturing plant		75
Sales delivery vans	100	
Manufacturing expenses	34	
Administration salaries	28	
Stocks		
Raw materials 1 January 19X0	13	
Finished goods	28	
General administration	11	
Rent	24	
Rates	16	
Debtors	56	
Cash	24	
Creditors		38
Wages delivery van drivers	30	
Drawings	36	
Long-term loan		120
Light, heat and power	28	
Vehicle running expense	13	
Advertising	23	
Bad debts	4	
	843	843

The following information is available:

1 Stock as at 31 December 19X0

   Raw materials   15

   Finished goods   33

2 Depreciate plant on straight-line basis, assuming a life of ten years and residual value of 14,000.

3 Delivery vans depreciate, assuming three years and residual value of 25,000.

4 75% of rent, rates and heat, light and power relate to manufacturing activity, the balance is for administration.

Required:

Prepare a manufacturing, trading, profit and loss account for year ending 31 December 19X0 and a balance sheet at that date.

Feedback

8.11 Your manufacturing, trading project and loss account and balance sheet should agree with these:

Ambergate
Manufacturing, trading profit and loss account
for year ending 31 December 19X0

	£000s	£000s
O/S raw materials	13	
Add purchases	126	
	139	
Less closing stock of raw materials	15	
Cost of raw materials consumed	124	
Add manufacturing wages	73	
Prime cost	197	
Add factory indirect costs		
Depreciation $\frac{164 - 14}{10}$	15	
Rent 24 x 75%	18	
Expenses	34	
Rates 16 x 75%	12	
Light, heat and power 28 x 75%	21	
Cost of production	297	
Sales		500
O/S of finished goods	28	
Add cost of production	297	
	325	
Less closing stock of finished goods	33	
Cost of goods sold		292
Gross profit		208
Less expenses		
Interest	12	
Administration salaries	28	
General administration	11	
Rates 16 x 25%	4	
Wages delivery van drivers	30	
Light, heat and power 28 x 25%	7	
Vehicle running expenses	13	
Advertising	23	
Bad debt	4	
Rent 24 x 25%	6	
Depreciation vans $\frac{100 - 25}{3}$	25	
		163
Net profit		45

Balance sheet

	£ Cost	£ Dep.	£ NBV
Fixed assets			
Plant	164	90	74
Vehicles	100	25	75
	264	115	149

Current assets
Stocks (15 + 33) 48
Debtors 56
Cash 24
  128

Current liabilities
Creditors 38
Working capital 90
  239

Less: Long-term liabilities
Loan 120
  119

Capital 110
Add net profit 45
  155
Less drawings 36
  119

9 Summary

9.1 The application of stock valuation and work-in-progress should now be clear to you. You will have seen how they are worked out and what their effects are. You know why it is important to value the stock correctly and the consequences if it is not. We have also discussed SSAP 9 and you know why it is imposed and to what, in general terms, it relates to in accounting.

9.2 In addition you have seen how to construct a manufacturing account and work out prime costs and production costs. You have seen that the production cost replaces the purchases figure in the trading account of a manufacturer.

Self-assessment questions

1. What is net realisable value?
2. Give the three methods of valuing stock.
3. Which SSAP deals with stocks?
4. Define a direct cost?
5. What types of stocks may we have in a manufacturing account?
6. What is the name given to general cost in the production process such as heat and light for the factory?
7. How is prime cost calculated?
8. What are added to prime cost in a manufacturing account to calculate the cost of production?
9. What is the figure transferred from the manufacturing account to the trading account?
10. Why are the totals of some costs divided and apportioned partly to the manufacturing account and partly to the profit and loss account?

Unit 17

Written Answer Questions

Objectives

By the end of this Unit, you will be able to:
- Answer essay-style questions set by the examiner.

1 Introduction

1.1 As mentioned in the introduction to your course, part of the exam will test your ability to explain various terms and your understanding of some of the basic ideas and terminology of accounting.

1.2 You should now be able to answer these questions. It is a very important part of the paper and by way of revision this Unit contains a series of questions which require written answers. Most of them are past examination questions, and will give you a good idea of what to expect in your exam. Remember, you can answer *both* questions in this section and earn up to 40 marks. Students usually find these questions quicker to answer than the accounting questions. So if you do answer both questions, you will be giving yourself more time per question for the accounting ones. Only do both, however, if you are quite sure of the answers.

1.3 As this Unit simply comprises questions for you to answer, there is no need for separate activities and self-assessment questions.

1.4 The figures in brackets show how many marks are available for each question.

1.5 Example answers to the questions are given at the end of the workbook.

2 Specimen written questions

Question 1
A long-established company has approached your bank for a loan, and has supported its request with a copy of its last set of published accounts. Explain the limitations of using these accounts alone in this situation. What additional information will you require as the lending banker? (20)

Question 2

(a) In the context of the preparation of a set of annual accounts, explain what you understand by the terms:

- accruals concept
- money measurement concept
- realisation concept. (6)

(b) A limited company is at an early stage of preparing its published annual accounts for the year to 31 December 1993. The directors are discussing whether, and if so how, the following information affects the accounts:

1 A piece of land which the company bought for 800,000 in 1985, and was recorded in the books at cost, was professionally valued in December 1993 at 1,500,000. The managing director thinks that the increase in value should be entered in the profit and loss account for 1993.

2 An employee was injured at work during 1993 and sued the company. The case was settled in January 1994 and the company had to pay the employee 16,000 in compensation. The managing director says that this can be ignored when preparing the accounts for 1993.

3 A competitor offered to buy the entire company for 5,000,000 on 30 June 1993. At the time of the offer the company's net tangible assets were worth 4,500,000. The offer was rejected by all the shareholders as they considered it to be far too low, but the managing director considers that the value of goodwill should be included in the balance sheet.

4 The company bought the entire business of Jones & Co. for 300,000 on 31 December 1993. The tangible net assets acquired were professionally valued at 225,000 on the day of acquisition of Jones & Co. The managing director says that the tangible net assets should be valued at 300,000 in the balance sheet.

Required:

Taking each of the items separately:

(i) State which ONE of the concepts given in part (a) of this question is the most applicable; and (4)

(ii) Explain:

Why the Managing Director is wrong. (4)

The correct accounting treatment. (4)

The impact on the annual account of the correct accounting treatment. (2)

(Total 20 marks)

Question 3

(a) Define the term goodwill. Explain how it comes into existence and the benefit which a firm derives if it possesses goodwill. (6)

(b) Define the terms capital expenditure and revenue expenditure. (4)

(c) On 31 March 1992 General Ltd acquired as a going concern the business Trainer, as a sole trader, for a cash payment of 450,000. The assets taken over were valued at the following amounts:

	£000
Debtors	74
Freehold land and buildings	200
Stock	26
Goodwill	80
Motor vehicles	65
Cash	5
	450

Using the information set out above, identify those assets that represent capital expenditure. Describe two alternative methods by which the goodwill acquired could be treated in the accounts of General Ltd and explain their impact on the balance sheet of General Ltd. (10)

(Total 20 marks)

Question 4

(a) Describe **three** types of long-term finance which may be found in the balance sheet of a business. (6)

(b) Define the term over-trading and describe **four** symptoms of over-trading which may be found in a set of annual accounts of a limited company. Explain why these indicate that over-trading might have occurred. (10)

(c) Explain why it is important for a business to fund long-term applications of funds in long-term sources of funds. (4)

(Total 20 marks)

Question 5

(a) Define the accounting terms capital expenditure and revenue expenditure. (4)

(b) Why is it important to differentiate between capital expenditure and revenue expenditure? (2)

(c) For **each** of the following transactions

- identify whether it is revenue expenditure or capital expenditure; and
- describe its treatment in the final accounts for the year to 30 September 1993.

1 October 1992: The addition of a new automatic loader to an existing metal processing machine. (2)

2 September 1993: The replacement of a factory's existing wooden windows with new double glazed, plastic framed windows. (2)

3 October 1992: The purchase by a motor dealer of a van to deliver spare parts to customers. (2)

4 August 1993: The purchase by a motor dealer of a van to be sold to a customer in October 1993. (2)

5 October 1992: The purchase of a competitor's business at a cost of 250,000. The tangible fixed assets acquired were valued at 150,000 and stock at 50,000; no other tangible assets or liabilities of any kind were acquired. (6)

(Total 20 marks)

Question 6

(a) Explain why the published annual accounts of all limited companies have to be audited and briefly describe the responsibilities of the auditor. (4)

(b) A limited company, which is already a customer, has approached your bank for an increased overdraft facility. The request is supported by the company's most recent set of published accounts in which the auditors report contains no adverse comments. What are the limitations of the accounts provided, from the point of view of deciding whether to allow an increased overdraft? (16)

(Total 20 marks)

Question 7

(a) In the context of the double entry system of bookkeeping define the terms day book and trial balance and explain their use. (6)

(b) A trader sells some goods for cash. Explain how this transaction is recorded in the books account, starting at the stage of prime entry, and reflected in the final accounts of the company. (10)

(c) Give two example of post trial balance adjustments. Explain why it is necessary to make these adjustments to convert the trial balance into a set of annual accounts comprising a profit and loss account and balance sheet. (4)

(Total 20 marks)

3 Answers to specimen written questions

Question 1

3.1 In the actual exam, this question was generally well answered, although a lot of students would have benefited from reading it more thoroughly. The question is centred on the limitations of using a single set of published accounts as the basis for a lending decision; too often, answers dealt with accounting information in general, including such items as management accounts, or concentrated on the process of making the loan. Also, the question asks for details of additional information that would be required; many students did not deal with this aspect.

3.2 The limitations of published accounts are:

1 *They are subjective.* A number of different, equally valid, methods of valuation can be applied, for example, the depreciation charge can be calculated using either the straight-line method or reducing balance method. Accounting policies can be chosen in such a way as to put the results in a favourable light, while still complying with the requirement to show a true and fair view.

2 *They do not provide forecast information.* The payment of interest and capital will depend on future results. Past results may be a guide to the future, but proper forecast accounts are better.

3 *Timeliness.* The information contained in published accounts is out of date. They may refer to a period which ended some time ago, and a lot could have happened in the meantime.

4 *Use of historical cost.* The values in the published accounts are based on historical cost.

5 *There may be undisclosed assets.* The published balance sheet does not contain all of a firm's assets, for example, goodwill that the firm has built up

6 *Window dressing.* The company might have undertaken transactions to enhance the apparent strength of the balance sheet, for example, a loan might be raised just prior to the accounting date and repaid soon after, thus for a short time, enhancing liquidity.

7 *Off balance sheet finance.* It is possible to fund some operations in such a way that there is no indication of the liability on the balance sheet.

3.3 The additional information which the banker would require includes:

1. A set of forecast accounts. These should include a cash flow forecast, profit and loss account and balance sheet.

2. Up to date management accounts are needed to show what has happened in the interval between the published accounts and the date of the loan request. Both the profit and loss account and balance sheet should be requested.

3. Current details of all assets and liabilities are available from the management accounts, but these are based on historical cost. Current valuations of assets should be obtained, together with details of any loans which are secured on them.

Question 2

3.4 This question was generally answered well, although students who were unable to explain the accounting concepts in part (a) tended to have difficulty applying them in part (b). The main difficulty with the definitions in part (a) was with accruals, where explanations were limited to the context of adjusting for specific accrual, as is done with heat and light in question 1. This error reflects a lack of familiarity with the terminology.

(a) *Accruals concept*: Revenues and costs are recognised when the economic event takes place and not at the time of the related cash flow.

Money measurement concept: Business assets are only reported in the balance sheet if their value can be measured in money terms with a reasonable degree of precision.

Realisation concept: Revenue is recorded as earned only when a sale has taken place, either for cash or on credit terms. No recognition is given to profit which has not been realised.

(b)

(i) The concept applicable to each part is:

1. Realisation
2. Accruals
3. Money measurement
4. Money measurement.

(ii) The reasons why the managing director is wrong, the correct accounting treatment and the impact on the annual accounts are:

1. The increase in value is 700,000, but this cannot be entered in the profit and loss account as the managing director wishes because it has not been realised.

    A correct treatment is to include the increase in value in the balance sheet using a revaluation reserve. The annual accounts would show the value of land in fixed assets increased by 700,000 included as part of equity.

2. Although the settlement took place in 1994, the event to which it relates occurred in 1993 and so the managing director is wrong to suggest that it can be ignored. The resulting loss was established in sufficient time to be included in the 1993 accounts, and so the accruals concept is applied.

The effect is to reduce 1993 profits by 16,000 and introduce a corresponding accrual in the closing balance sheet as part of current liabilities.

3. The managing director is wrong to suggest that the value of goodwill be included in the annual accounts as it is not purchased goodwill. The sum offered, values goodwill at 500,000, but the offer was rejected as too low, and so this sets a value for goodwill which is lower than that expected by the shareholders. No indication is given of the true worth of the company as a whole, and so no entry can be made in the accounts for goodwill because it is not capable of money measurement. Even if it were possible to find a value for the company as a whole, the goodwill element could not be included in the accounts as the Managing Director thinks should be done. As a result, this has no impact on the annual accounts other than that it must not be included.

4. The managing director is wrong to suggest altering the value of the tangible net assets as this ignores the fact that the cost of the acquired business includes goodwill. In this case, the value of goodwill can be found by deducting the value of the tangible net assets from the value of the company as a whole, giving a value of 75,000. The goodwill has been the subject of a monetary transaction and so is entered in the books; it is purchased goodwill. Therefore, the money measurement concept has been satisfied. It gives rise to a debit balance of 75,000 and the accounting policy of how to deal with it in the annual accounts has to be decided; the choice lies between immediate write off to reserves or capitalisation and amortisation.

Question 3

(a) You should have noted that this contains three separate elements: define goodwill; explain how it comes into existence; and explain the benefit it gives a firm. Care should be taken to ensure that each of these is covered in the answer, as follows:

- Goodwill is the amount by which the value of a whole firm as a going concern exceeds the value of its separate tangible assets.

- Goodwill comes into existence over the years from the creation of a good name and reputation.

- The firm benefits from the posession of goodwill as it enables it to earn a profit greater than would be expected from the tangible assets alone.

(b) This part was generally answered well. The main errors were made by students who had not learned the correct definitions, and, for example, tried to relate capital expenditure to that made from money in the capital account. The correct definitions are:

- *Capital expenditure* is that made on fixed assets. These are expected to be used up within the business and not resold in the normal course of trade. Their life expectancy exceeds one year.

- *Revenue expenditure* is made on short-lived assets and expenses which are part of the trading activity of the business. Their life expectancy is less than one year.

(c) Most students correctly identified land and motor vehicles as fixed assets; fewer included goodwill. Reference to the above definitions shows that goodwill has all the characteristics of a fixed asset. The section on describing how to deal with the goodwill in the accounts was very badly answered. It should be noted that the goodwill is purchased by a limited company, General Ltd, and so bringing the use of partners' capital accounts into the description of how it could be treated cannot be correct.

Capital expenditure: land, motor vehicles, goodwill.

The two methods of dealing with goodwill are:

1 *Capitalise and amortise*. The value of goodwill is entered in the balance sheet as a fixed asset and this is written off through the profit and loss account over its estimated life. It must not be carried as a permanent balance. Over the years the value in the balance sheet declines to zero.

2 *Write off immediately*. The purchase of goodwill is capital expenditure, but a permissible, and preferred, accounting treatment is to write it off immediately on acquisition. Therefore under this approach, no value appears in the balance sheet, and reserves are reduced by the value of goodwill acquired.

Question 4

(a) Most students managed to state three sources of long-term finance, but the question asks for them to be described. There are a number of possible sources for which marks were given, but the three main ones are:

1 *Owners' capital introduced*: This is the amount invested by the owners in a business. It does not receive a fixed return, but the owners are entitled to any profits made.

2 *Debentures and loans*: These are debts due by the firm, and are of a long-term nature. They usually carry a fixed rate of interest and have set repayment terms.

3 *Retained profits/funds generated from operations*: These comprise net profit plus depreciation and are available to management to invest in long-term assets. The retained profits are added to owners' capital, and the depreciation charge effectively sets aside some profit to allow for the fact that the value of fixed assets has declined as a result of being used in the business.

(b) This produced some interesting, but incorrect guesses, including some which, on reflection, students must have known were wrong, for example, over-trading is selling too much and a firm over-trades when it sells more than would be accepted as normal. Based on definitions like these, the identification of symptoms provokes even greater ingenuity. The result of attempting a question when the answer to one part is not known means that the 10 marks allocated for this section are lost. The correct answer is:

- Over-trading is a condition that arises when a company attempts to do too much too quickly and, as a result, fails to maintain a satisfactory balance between profit maximisation and financial stability. Symptoms, of which four were to be given, include:

- heavy expenditure on fixed assets

- a fall in cash especially if to an overdraft position

- a less liquid structure of current assets

- a sharp rise in creditors

- poor working capital and liquidity ratios

- excessive turnover relative to the capital base.

    Over-trading results when short-term funds are used to finance long-term assets. Each of these symptoms show that this might be happening, but it is necessary for both conditions to be present.

(c) The objective of management is to earn profits, but this must be done while maintaining financial stability, i.e. the firm must be able to meet its debts as they fall due. If long-term applications are not funded from long-term sources, it means that short-term sources must have been used, and this may have used up available liquid funds. If this has happened, then an overdraft may arise and short-term creditors remain unpaid. The next step is likely to be a cut-off of supplies and/or a termination of overdraft facilities.

Question 5

This involves the definition of two terms and their subsequent application to practical examples. In answer to the definitions required in part (a), it is not enough simply to give examples, although these can be used to reinforce an answer.

This question was well answered. The main problem arose with the last part of section (c). It is possible for a single transaction to involve both revenue and capital items, and so each aspect is dealt with separately. A single categorisation of capital or revenue cannot be made for the whole amount.

Correct answers contained the following:

(a) *Capital expenditure* is expenditure on the long-term fabric of the enterprise; it enhances its long-term ability to earn profits. For example, buildings or plant and machinery.

Revenue expenditure is expenditure on the day–to–day running of the business; it maintains its capacity. For example, purchases and wages.

(b) It is important to differentiate between revenue and capital expenditure, as capital expenditure is entered in the balance sheet as part of fixed assets, and if necessary depreciated, while revenue expenditure is written off in the profit and loss account at the time it is incurred.

(c)

1 This is capital expenditure as it is long-term improvement to the ability of the firm to make profits. Therefore, it is included under fixed assets and depreciated.

2 This is an improvement to a fixed asset, and so should be capitalised as part of the cost of buildings and depreciated. Theoretically, the book value of the wooden windows at the time of their replacement should be deducted for the book value of the building; the identification of a net book value is likely to present practical problems.

3 This is capital expenditure as the van is not acquired with the intention of resale in the normal course of trade. It should be included in the balance sheet as a fixed asset and depreciated.

4 This is revenue expenditure. It would appear as stock at cost in the accounts until it is sold.

5 The fixed assets are capital expenditure and so are included under this in the balance sheet and depreciated. The stock is revenue expenditure and is included as part of current assets in the balance sheet until sold, when it is transferred to the trading and profit and loss account as part of the cost of goods sold. The balance of 50,000 is goodwill; this is a fixed asset and should either be written off directly to reserves or treated as fixed assets and depreciated.

Question 6

The auditor's responsibility is to comment on whether the accounts show a true and fair view. Auditors do not, as was suggested by many students, have to comment on the progress and position of the company revealed by the accounts. The answer to the first part of the question is:

(a) The published accounts of all limited companies have to be audited because it is a legal requirement. The audit is carried out so that the auditor, who is independent of the company, can report to shareholders on whether the accounts give a true and fair view of the company's results and position. A secondary purpose of the audit is to check whether errors have been made or fraud taken place; these are only picked up if they are uncovered as part of routine audit procedures.

The second part of the question deals with the limitations of published accounts in the context of deciding whether to grant an increased overdraft. The assumption, when a firm is granted an increase in its overdraft facility, is that it will be able to pay the interest on it, and, eventually, repay the amount borrowed. The limitations of the published accounts for the purpose of deciding whether to grant an increase in a firm's overdraft facility are:

(b)

1. *Subjective judgement* is used to value assets, for example, deciding on the depreciation policy. This results in arbitrary valuations of fixed assets.

2. *Lack of forecast information*, as the accounts report what has happened in the past. This is not necessarily a reliable guide to the future. The overdraft and interest will have to be repaid by future cash inflows.

3. *Out of date information* arises because the accounts cover a period which ended a number of months previously.

4. *Historical costs* are used, and so the assets are not reported at their current values.

5. *Undisclosed assets*, such as goodwill, may exist and are not disclosed in the balance sheet. The result is that the full extent of the ability of the company to meet its obligations is not shown.

6. *Lack of sufficiently detailed segmental information* means that seasonal factors are not clear, nor the impact of individual products or locations.

Question 7

The following answer to part (b) provides an outline, but many alternative approaches were equally acceptable. The basic requirement is to describe how the data relating to the transaction is captured, recorded, processed and reported. Similarly, there are many possible correct answers to part (c), and these were all given due credit. The answer provided below does not attempt to cover all possibilities, but is intended to indicate the outline of an answer which would attract the marks allocated.

(a) *Day book*: The day-to-day record of transactions (sales, purchases, etc.). It is periodically totalled to provide the input to the double entry system.

Trial balance: A list of debit and credit balances extracted from all the accounts of the business. It is used as the basis for preparing final accounts and checking the arithmetic accuracy of the books.

(b) The steps are:

1 The receipt of cash is entered in the cash book in the sales column. In this case the cash book is the day book.

2 At regular intervals, the cash book columns are totalled and the total of the sales column entered as credit in the Sales account.

3 At the end of the accounting year, the balances are extracted from the cash account and the sales account and entered in the trial balance.

4 The trial balance is adjusted to form the basis from which the final accounts are prepared.

5 In the final accounts, the cash is shown in the balance sheet and sales in the trading and profit and loss account.

(c) It is necessary to adjust the trial balance because it does not contain all of the information which is to be reflected in the accounts. A number of events are not automatically recorded by the day-to-day accounting system, such as: depreciation, accruals, prepayments, bad debts.

4 Summary

4.1 In this Unit you have seen the importance of being able to explain various elements of accounting and have had some practice in this area. You should also have realised how important it is to have grasped the underlying concepts of accounting as well as to be able to explain these to the examiner.

Unit 18

Past Paper Questions – Numerical

Objectives

By the end of this Unit you will be able to:

- deal more proficiently with numerical examination questions.

1 Introduction

1.1 To be successful in your examination, it is not enough that you understand the principles of accounting. You must also be able to:

- apply and discuss the principles
- work with accuracy and speed.

1.2 Practice on past examination questions is very important to ensure that you make the most effective use of your studies. This Unit simply comprises questions for you to answer together with suggested answers. You should ensure that by the time you complete this Unit and further revision, you are able to tackle past papers within the given time and under examination conditions.

1.3 There are no activities or self-assessment questions in this Unit.

2 Importance of practising past questions

2.1 One of the most important ways of preparing for any exam is by practice. This is particularly important for making sure you can work within the time constraints. In an accounting exam, since time is not always on your side, although you may be able to answer the questions, unless the basic theories come easily to you, you may find yourself falling behind the clock. Work through the following questions; they have been included here because they represent the types of questions most often asked.

2.2 Time yourself and see how long it takes. Bear in mind that 40 minutes should be the maximum time for a question, although at this stage you may take a little longer. In the exam you are recommended to do as much as you can within this time and then go on to the next question. If something doesn't quite balance, don't waste valuable time looking for the difference, you could be scoring marks on other questions. Leave some space and go back to the question later if you have the time.

3 Past examination questions – numerical

Question 1

3.1 Wave and Trough run a shop as partners. The following is the trial balance extracted from the firm's ledger at 30 June 1990:

	£	£
Capital 30 June 1989:		
Wave		90,000
Trough		75,000
Drawings:		
Wave	16,000	
Trough	15,800	
Current account balances at 30 June 1989:		
Wave	1,000	
Trough		10,600
Sales		611,300
Purchases	426,100	
Stock at 30 June 1989	35,500	
Rates on premises	15,000	
Wages	36,900	
Motor expenses	6,300	
Land and buildings at cost	134,000	
Motor vehicle:		
at cost	20,000	
accumulated depreciation at 30 June 1989		3,000
Fixtures and fittings:		
at cost	55,200	
accumulated depreciation at 30 June 1989		10,000
Bank		15,100
Debtors and creditors	101,800	35,500
Bank charges and interest	3,600	
Advertising	21,200	
Discounts allowed and received	9,800	2,700
Long-term loan at 10%		50,000
Interest on long-term loan	5,000	
	903,200	903,200

3.2 You are given the following additional information:

1 Stock at 30 June 1990 was valued at 42,700.

2 The rates account contains a payment of 8,000 made in April 1990 for the six months to 30 September 1990.

3 Some advertising was undertaken in April 1990, and the invoice for 4,300 was received in July. This is not included in the trial balance.

4 During the year to 30 June 1990, Wave took goods for his own use which cost 1,500. No record of this was made in the firm's books.

5 The motor vehicle is depreciated on the straight-line basis assuming a life of ten years and a residual value of 2,000.

   The fixtures and fittings are also depreciated on the straight-line basis assuming a life of ten years and a residual value of 5,200.

6 The partners agree that profit and losses should be shared equally, after giving each partner interest on his capital account balance of 12% a year and an annual salary of 20,000 to Wave and 30,000 to Trough.

7 Capital account balances are to remain unchanged.

Required:
Prepare the trading profit and loss account of Wave and Trough for the year to 30 June 1990 and the Balance Sheet at that date.

(Total 20 marks)
(CIB past question)

Question 2

3.2 From the following information, prepare a cash flow statement for the year ended 30 April 1989.

The company deals in television sets, both selling and hiring them.

Profit and loss accounts year ended 30 April

	1989 £	1989 £	1988 £	1988 £
Net profit for the year after charging:		21,871		13,550
Depreciation on shop fittings	5,942		4,102	
Depreciation on TV sets for rental	10,537		8,275	
Depreciation on motor vehicles	5,070		4,510	
Directors' remuneration	25,000		24,000	
Bank charges	691		1,209	
Provision for bad debts	1,340		696	
Less provision for corporation tax on the profits of the year		5,100		4,300
		16,771		9,250
Profit on sale of motor vehicles		285		–
Loss on sale of TV sets for rental		–		205
		17,056		9,045
Less dividends proposed		1,500		1,000
		15,556		8,045
Retained profits brought forward		25,142		17,097
		40,698		25,142
Transfer to general reserve		10,000		–
Retained profits carried forward		30,698		25,142

Note: In the year ended 30 April 1988, TV sets for rental were sold for 750. These had originally cost 8,200 and had been written down to 955.

In the year ended 30 April 1989, motor vehicles were sold for 4,250. These had originally cost 10,500 and had been written down to 3,965.

Balance sheets at 30 April

	1989 £	1989 £	1988 £	1988 £
Fixed assets				
Shop fittings at cost	38,189		33,189	
Less aggregate depreciation	15,362	22,827	9,420	23,769
TV sets for rental at cost	39,250		39,250	
Less aggregate depreciation	28,712	10,538	18,175	21,075
Motor vehicles at cost	38,200		27,200	
Less aggregate depreciation	6,670	31,530	8,135	19,065
		64,895		63,909
Current assets				
Stock of TV sets for sale	24,107		19,206	
Debtors	10,134		12,101	
Prepaid expenses	1,786		952	
Cash at bank	11,200		–	
	47,227		32,259	
Less current liabilities				
Creditors	14,019		17,803	
Accrued expenses	805		737	
Bank overdraft	–		7,186	
Provision for corporation tax	5,100		4,300	
Proposed dividends	1,500		1,000	
	21,424	25,803	31,026	1,233
		90,698		65,142
Share capital and reserves				
Issued share capital	30,000		25,000	
Share premium account	10,000		5,000	
General reserve	20,000		10,000	
Profit and loss account	30,698	90,698	25,142	65,142

(Total 20 marks)

(CIB past question)

Question 3

3.3 Steel Ltd and Carbon Ltd are two independent retail businesses which have traded in the same two products, A and B, for several years. The following information has been extracted from their draft annual accounts for the year to 31 March 1994:

	Steel £000	Carbon £000
Sales - Product A	400	600
Sales - Product B	600	400
Cost of goods sold (variable) - Product A	200	300
Cost of goods sold (variable) - Product B	450	300
Stock at 31 March 1994 - Product A	75	48
Stock at 31 March 1994 - Product B	45	90
Debtors at 31 March 1994	126	154
Creditors at 31 March 1994	49	117
General expenses for the year to 31 March 1994 (Note 1)	210	225
Fixed assets at cost 31 March 1994	480	360
Accumulated depreciation at 31 March 1994	144	108
Cash and bank balance 31 March 1994	30	6
Share capital (ordinary shares of 1 each)	220	150
10% Debentures repayable 1999	150	0
Profit and loss account balance at 31 March 1993	53	108

Notes:

1 General expenses are all fixed, and the balances shown include debenture interest and depreciation for the year to 31 March 1994.

2 The companies had no revenue, expenses, assets or liabilities other than those given above and the dividend detailed in note 3.

3 Both companies decide to declare a dividend of 10 pence per share for the year to 31 March 1994.

Required:

(a) Prepare summary trading and profit and loss accounts for each company separately for the year to 31 March 1994 in a format which provides maximum information. Your answers should show clearly the contribution made by each product and the profit retained by each company for the year. (5)

(b) Prepare the balance sheet of each company separately as at 31 March 1994. (5)

(c) Explain and evaluate the impact on each of the companies of a fall of 25% in the sales of product A, combined with a fall of 25% in the sales of product B. (10)

(Total 20 marks)

Note: Your answers do not have to be in a form suitable for publication.

Question 4

3.4 David owns a fruiterer's shop and his annual accounting date is 30 September. David's balance sheet at 30 September 1988 was as follows:

Balance Sheet – 30 September 1988

	£	£
Leasehold shop at cost	12,100	
Less: deprecation	8,150	
		3,950
Shop equipment at cost	19,634	
Less: depreciation	11,585	
		8,049
		11,999
Stock	931	
Trade debtors	358	
Deposit account	6,412	
	7,701	
Less:		
Trade creditors	2,150	
Bank overdraft	32	
	2,182	
		5,519
		17,518
Financed by:		
Capital account		17,518

David's bank account for the year to 30 September 1989 may be summarised as follows:

Bank current account

	£		£
Takings paid to bank	60,205	Balance 1 October 1988	32
Interest on deposit account	428	Payments to suppliers	37,014
		Wages	10,398
		Rent and rates	7,500
		Heating and lighting	1,201
		Bank charges	314
		Transfer to bank deposit account	500
		Sundry trade expenses	1,792
		Personal drawings	1,047
		Balance 30 September 1989	835
	60,633		60,633

Other information relating to the year ended 30 September 1989 is given below.

1. All cash takings had been paid into the bank with the exception of 5,500 which David withheld for personal expenditure.

2. At 30 September 1989 stock was valued at 1,240; debtors amounted to 241; David owed his suppliers 786.

3. Depreciation to be charged for the year is to be 1,210 in respect of the leasehold shop, and 1,422 in respect of the shop equipment.

4. At 30 September 1989 rent and rates were prepaid by 824, and electricity charges accrued were 210.

Required:

(a) A trading and profit and loss account for the year ended 30 September 1989. (10)

(b) A balance sheet at 30 September 1989. (10)

(Total 20 marks)
(CIB past question)

Question 5

3.5 Tower is a sole trader who owns a retail shop. The trial balance extracted from the firm's ledger at 31 December 1991 is:

	£000	£000
Capital at 1 January 1991		148
Loan from the finance company		50
Freehold premises at cost	108	
Fixtures and fittings at cost	25	
Accumulated depreciation on fixtures and fittings at 1 January 1991		10
Stock at 1 January 1991	125	
Purchases	620	
Wages and salaries	31	
Rates	16	
Debtors	64	
Sales		800
Creditors		38
Delivery expenses	7	
Bank		7
Bank interest	1	
Bank charges	2	
Heat, light and power	9	
Drawings	24	
General expenses	21	
	1,053	1,053

The following information is relevant:

1 During the year to 31 December 1991, Tower withdrew stock which had cost 3,000 for his personal use. This is not reflected in the above trial balance.

2 No depreciation is charged on freehold property.

3 Stock at 31 December 1991 was valued at 136,000.

4 During the year to 31 December 1991 additional fixtures and fittings were purchased at a cost of 5,000. This was, in error, entered in the purchases account.

5 Fixtures and fittings are to be depreciated on the reducing balance basis using an annual rate of 40%.

6 On 31 December 1991, by agreement with Tower, a customer who had paid for them, returned the goods. Their selling price was 16,000 and they had cost Tower 10,000. Their return is not reflected in the above trial balance, but they have been included in closing stock at a value of 16,000.

7 Bad debts of 4,000 are to be written off, and a general provision for doubtful debts of 9,000 created.

8   At 31 December 1991 bank interest and bank charges outstanding, and not yet accrued, amounted to 1,000 and 2,000 respectively, and 2,000 of rates had to be paid in advance.

9   The loan from the finance company was taken out in 1987 and carries an annual interest charge of 12%, which is paid on 1 January each year in respect of the previous year.

Required:
Prepare the trading and profit and loss account of Tower for the year to 31 December 1991 and the balance sheet at that date. The balance sheet should disclose the values of fixed assets, current assets, current liabilities, working capital and Towers capital at 31 December 1991.

(Total 20 marks)

Question 6

3.6   Plato Ltd started business on 1 January 1991. The company has two separate divisions, one manufactures a product called Aristo and the other a product called Tottle. The following information is provided about the company:

	Aristo	Tottle
Plant purchased 1 January 1991:		
Cost	£1,000,000	£250,000
Residual value at end of life	£100,000	£50,000
Life	10 years	10 years
Maximum annual output	50,000 units	70,000 units
Production and sales (in units) for the year to 31 December:		
1991 (actual)	30,000	20,000
1992 (actual)	40,000	30,000
1993 (forecast)	50,000	40,000
Selling price per unit	£9.00	£9.50
Material cost per unit (variable)	£1.80	£1.60
Labour cost per unit (variable)	£2.20	£0.90
Annual fixed costs (excluding depreciation)	£100,000	£92,000
Annual depreciation charge	£90,000	£20,000

The company uses straight-line depreciation. There were no stocks of any kind held at the end of any of the years.

The managers of the company are satisfied that production and sales of both products will grow by 10,000 units in 1994. The division producing Aristo will be at full capacity by the end of 1993, and the further increase in the demand for Aristo during 1994 can be met in either of two ways:

1   Buy the finished products from Hume Ltd for 8,000 per unit and resell them. No further processing would need to be done by Plato.

2   Double the capacity of the Aristo division by purchasing an additional set of fixed assets. These would be identical in all respects to those purchased on 1 January 1991.

The fixed costs excluding depreciation would not be affected by either course of action.

Required:

(a) Prepare, in columnar format, the separate profit and loss accounts for the two products for each of the three years to 31 December 1993. (6)

(b) Calculate the break even points of Aristo and Tottle in 1991, in terms of the number of units to be sold. (4)

(c) Discuss the relative profitability of the two products. (4)

(d) Prepare a simple comparison of the alternatives which are available to meet the anticipated additional demand for Aristo in 1994. You should include appropriate calculations in your answers, and restrict your discussion to 1994. (6)

(Total 20 marks)

Question 7

3.7 Ruby, Pearl and Opal started trading in partnership on 1 October 1993. They decided to draw up a draft trading and profit and loss account for the year to September 1994 and a balance sheet at that date. The resulting balance sheet is as follows:

Balance sheet

	£	£
Fixed assets at cost		110,000
Less accumulated depreciation		20,000
		90,000
Stock	50,000	
Trade debtors	60,000	
Cash	1,000	
	111,000	
Trade creditors	40,000	
		71,000
		161,000
Financed by:		
Capital introduced:		
Ruby		70,000
Pearl		50,000
		120,000
Profit for the year		41,000
		161,000

You are provided with the following additional information:

1. The accounts do not reflect the fact that Opal introduced capital on 1 October 1993 in the form of premises, valued at 30,000, and a car valued at 10,000. The premises are not to be depreciated, but the car is expected to have a residual value of 2,000 at the end of its life of four years. Straight-line depreciation is to be used.

2. Business rates of 6,000 were paid on 28 September 1994; this payment is for the six months to 31 March 1995.

3. A debt of 1,000, included in the balance sheet, is expected to prove bad.

4. The partners drew the following amounts of cash during the year, which were recorded in the wages account and taken into consideration when calculating the profit figure:

	£
Ruby	10,000
Pearl	15,000
Opal	13,000

5. It is the partners intention to maintain capital and current accounts; the capital accounts are to contain only the value of capital introduced at the start of the business.

6. The partners are considering sharing profit equally, after allowing for interest of 10% on capital accounts and a salary of 9,000 for Ruby, 6,000 for Pearl and 12,000 for Opal.

Required:

(a) Calculate the adjusted trading profit of the Ruby, Pearl and Opal partnership for the year to 30 September 1994 and show its division between partners. (7)

(b) Prepare the balance sheet of the Ruby, Pearl and Opal partnership, showing a separate current account for each partner. (9)

(c) Explain how profit would be divided between the partners if no agreement were drawn up to deal with this matter. (4)

(Total 20 marks)

Question 8

3.8 Mr Matrix set up business on 1 July 1990 as a window cleaner, and on that day opened a bank account into which he paid 7,000 as capital. During the year to 31 June 1991 the following took place:

1 On 1 July 1990 he bought a second-hand van for 6,000 and a set of ladders for 550.

2 On 5 July 1990 he paid 450 to have a sign painted on the sides of the van, which would last for the life of the van.

3 During the year to 31 June 1991 he received cash from customers of 15,000, and he paid by cheque: 1,025 for sundry materials: 1,500 for motor expenses: and 2,500 for casual labour. He withdrew 750 per month for his own use.

4 At 30 June 1990 he was owed 750 by an industrial customer. He himself owed 75 for sundry materials and 85 for motor expenses. He valued the van and ladders at 5,310 and 405 respectively after charging depreciation for the year.

5 All cash receipts were immediately paid into the bank, and all payments were made by cheque. On 30 June 1991 he had issued cheques totalling 890 which had not yet appeared on the bank statements. The last day's takings of 50 (included in the total takings for the year), although banked immediately and entered in the cash book, did not appear on the bank statement until 1 July 1991.

Required:

(a) Prepare the cash account of Mr Matrix's business for the year to 30 June 1991. (4)

(b) Calculate the balance which appears on the firm's bank statement at 10 June 1991, and reconcile it with the balance on the cash account prepared in answer to part (a) of this question. (2)

(c) Mr Matrix estimates that the van will last five years and have a residual value at the end of that time of 750. Identify and explain which depreciation policy Mr Matrix is using. (2)

(d) Prepare Mr Matrix's profit and loss account for the year to 30 June 1991 and the balance sheet as at that date. (12)

(Total 20 marks)

Question 9

3.9 Mr Sutol rented a shop and started trading on 1 January 1991 under the name Sutol & Co. He did not keep any accounting records, and has asked you to help him calculate the firm's profit for 1991 and its position at the year end. You have asked him to provide you with details of assets and liabilities and in response he has given you the following items of information:

1. I opened a business bank account on 1 January and transferred into it 10,000 from my personal current account which I had won as a premium bond prize. This left a balance of 530 on my personal account.

2. On 1 January I purchased a delivery van for 8,000; the value of this on 31 December was about 6,000. I have kept my car for personal use; this was worth 3,000 on 1 January and, at that time, had about three years life left.

3. During the year I had to arrange an overdraft for the business, and used my house as security. As I bought my house some time ago for 45,000, the bank asked me to have it valued, and I was pleased to find out that it is now worth 125,000, although I still owe the building society 12,000 on its mortgage.

4. I managed to reduce the firm's overdraft on 1 July as my rich uncle lent the firm 4,000 which was paid into the business bank account. We agreed that he will be paid 6% annual interest on the loan, with the first payment being made on 30 June 1992.

5. 1991 must have been my lucky year as I won another premium bond prize, although this time it was only 1,000, which I paid into the business bank account.

6. During 1991 I took 15,000 in cash from the business for living expenses.

7. At 31 December 1991 I reckon that the assets and liabilities not mentioned above were:

	£
Bank overdraft	2,700
Cash in personal bank account	450
Trading stock	3,300
Electricity due on business premises	70
Electricity due on house	50
Rates prepaid on business premises	260
Creditors for trading purchases	1,125
Debtors for sales	2,500
Bank interest on overdraft and charges due	110

Required:

(a) Define the term entity concept and explain its effect on the preparation of accounting reports. Illustrate your answer using the information numbered 1 to 6 given above. (10)

(b) Prepare the balance sheet of Sutol & Co. at 31 December 1991, showing clearly the firm's profit for 1991. (10)

(Total 20 marks)

Question 10

3.10 The directors of Metal Ltd plan to increase the size of the company in the latter half of 1994 to about twice its current size. They have approached the bank for an overdraft facility to finance any short-term needs for funds. The bank has requested a detailed monthly cash flow forecast showing the impact of the expansion plans.

You have been provided with the following information:

1

Forecast balance sheet at 30 June 1994

	£000	£000
Fixed assets at cost		500
Less: accumulated depreciation		250
		250
Stock	110	
Debtors	160	
Cash	5	
	275	
Less: trade creditors	160	
Working capital		115
		365
Financed by:		
ordinary shares of 1 each		150
profit and loss account		215
		365

2 Monthly sales are expected to be:

	£000
July 1994	260
August 1994	260
September 1994	300
October 1994	450
November 1994	500
December 1994	600

Half of the company's customers take one month's credit, the other half pay in cash.

3 The company calculates the selling price of its goods by adding 100% to its cost, i.e. an item which cost the company 100 is sold for 200.

Each month the company purchases enough goods to replace the goods sold during the month, and one month's credit is received from suppliers.

4 The following changes in stock levels are planned:

	£000
October 1994 increase	50
November 1994 increase	40
December 1994 increase	20

5 In July, August and September 1994 the company will make payments in respect of:

	£000
Wages and salaries	90
General expenses	26

As a result of the expansion, both of these will increase by 50% for October 1994 and remain at this higher level for the rest of the year.

6 During the period of the forecast, other transactions are expected to be:

	£000
(a) Purchase of fixed assets – paid August	475
(b) Issue 10% debenture – received July	400
The interest is payable annually in arrears.	
(c) Advertising related to the expansion paid:	
– September	50
– October	35
– November	15

Required:

(a) Prepare a monthly cash flow forecast for Metal Ltd for the six months to 31 December 1994. You should use a columnar format and show clearly the balance at the end of each month. (12)

(b) Comment on the proposed expansion, and the expected working capital position of the company on 31 December 1994. (8)

(Total 20 marks)

4 Suggested answers to past examination questions – numerical

Question 1

Wave and Trough Partnership
Trading and profit and loss account for the year to 30 June 1990

		£	£
Sales			611,300
Opening stock		35,500	
Purchases		426,100	
Stock drawings		-1,500	
Closing stock		-42,700	
Cost of goods sold			417,400
Gross profit			193,900
Wages		36,900	
Rates (15,000 - 4,000)		11,000	
Motor expenses		6,300	
Depreciation:			
Motor vehicle		3,000	
Fixtures and fittings		5,000	
Bank charges		3,600	
Advertising (21,200 + 4,300)		25,500	
Discounts allowed		9,800	
Loan interest		5,000	
			106,100
			87,800
Discounts received			2,700
Net profit			90,500
Appropriation			
Interest:	Wave	10,800	
	Trough	9,000	
Salary:	Wave	20,000	
	Trough	30,000	
Residue:	Wave	10,350	
	Trough	10,350	
			90,500

Wave and Trough Partnership
Balance Sheet at 30 June 1990

	£	£	£
Fixed Assets			
Freehold land at cost		134,000	
Motor vehicle at cost	20,000		
Less accumulated depreciation	6,000		
		14,000	
Fixtures and fittings at cost	55,200		
Less accumulated depreciation	15,000		
		40,200	
		188,200	
Current assets			
Stock	42,700		
Debtors	101,800		
Prepayment	4,000		
	148,500		
Current liabilities			
Creditors	35,500		
Overdraft	15,100		
Accrual	4,300		
	54,900		
Working capital		93,600	
		281,800	
Less: loan		50,000	
		231,800	

Financed by:	Wave	Trough	Total
Capital accounts	90,000	75,000	165,000
Current accounts			
Balance	(1,000)	10,600	
Stock drawings	(1,500)	–	
Interest	10,800	9,000	
Salary	20,000	30,000	
Residue	10,350	10,350	
Drawings	(16,000)	(15,800)	
	22,650	44,150	66,800
			231,800

Question 2

Cash flow statement for year ending 30 April 1989

	£	£
Operating activities		
Net profit		21,871
Depreciation	5,942	
	10,537	
	5,070	
		21,549
		43,420
Increase in stock	(4,901)	
Decrease in debtors	1,967	
Increase in prepayments	(834)	
Decrease in creditors	(3,784)	
Increase in accruals	68	
		(7,484)
Net cash inflow from operating activities		35,936
Returns on investments and financing		
Dividends paid		(1,000)
		34,936
Taxation		
Taxation paid		(4,300)
		30,636
Investing activities		
Purchase of shop fittings	(5,000)	
Purchase of motor vehicles	(21,500)	
Net cash outflow before financing	4,250	
		(22,250)
Net cash flow before financing		8,386
Financing		
Issue of shares (5,000 + 5,000)		10,000
Increase in bank/cash		18,386

Changes in bank/cash

1989 cash	11,200	
Balance at 31 December 19X8	(7,186)	
Net cash inflow	18,386	

Workings re motor vehicles (not essential to be shown)

	Cost £	Aggregate depreciation £
B/fwd	27,200	8,135
Sales	(10,500)	(6,535)
	16,700	1,600
Purchases (balancing figure)	21,500	
Depreciation for year		5,070
Balance sheet 1989	38,200	6,670

Question 3

Question 3 gives details extracted from the draft accounts of two companies which have to be arranged into accounting statements. These are:

(a)

Summary trading and profit accounts for the year to 31 March 1994

	Steel A	Steel B	Carbon A	Carbon B
Sales	400	600	600	400
Variable cost of goods	200	450	300	300
Contribution	200	150	300	100
Combined contribution	350		400	
Fixed expenses	210		225	
Net profit	140		175	
Dividend	22		15	
Retained profit	118		160	

(b)
Balance sheet as at 31 March 1994

	£	£	£	£
Fixed assets: at cost		480		360
Less: accumulated depreciation		144		108
		336		252
Stock	120		138	
Debtors	126		154	
Cash	30		6	
	276		298	
Creditors	49		117	
Proposed dividend	22		15	
	71		132	
		205		166
		541		418
Debentures		150		0
		391		418
Financed by:				
Ordinary shares		220		150
Profit b/f	53		108	
Retained profit for year	118		160	
		171		268
		391		418

(c)
Evaluation

	Steel		Carbon	
	A	B	A	B
Sales	400	600	600	400
Sales 25%	300	450	450	300
Less Variable cost of sales	150	337.5	225	225
Revised contribution	150	112.5	225	75
Previous contribution	200	150.0	300	100
Loss of profit	50	37.5	75	25

Explanation

The impact on each of the companies of falls in sales of each of the products depends on the variable costs incurred for each product. Variable costs are those which change in direct proportion to changes in the level of activity levels and so can be ignored.

Variable costs are 50% of sales value for A (i.e. contribution 50%), and 75% for B (i.e. contribution 25%). Therefore, the company which relies more heavily on product A will suffer a greater fall in profit for a given fall in the level of activity.

A fall in the sales of A affects Carbon more than Steel, whereas a similar fall in sales of B affects Steel more than Carbon.

(d) Student errors

The main errors made by students were:

- failure to identify the separate result for product A and B.
- omitting the proposed dividend
- adjusting the figures given for cost of goods sold with the stock figures (presumably thinking the figures provided were purchases).
- in part (c) not dealing with the two requested aspects of explaining and evaluating.
- not appreciating the difference between fixed and variable costs when answering part (c).

Question 4

		£
Sales:	Cash banked	60,205
	Add takings not banked	5,500
	Less opening debtors	(358)
	Add closing debtors	241
Sales for year		65,588
Purchases:	Payments from bank	37,014
	Less opening creditors	(2,150)
	Add closing creditors	786
Purchases for year		35,650

These values can then be entered in the accounts.

Trading and profit and loss account for the year to 30 September 1989

	£	£
Sales		65,588
Purchases	35,650	
Add opening stock	931	
Less closing stock	(1,240)	
Cost of goods sold		35,341
Gross profit		30,247
Wages	10,398	
Rent and rates (7,500 824)	6,676	
Heat and light (1,201 + 210)	1,411	
Bank charges	314	
Sundry expenses	1,792	
Depreciation: leasehold premises	1,210	
equipment	1,422	
		23,223
Profit on trading		7,024
Add bank interest		428
Net profit		7,452

Balance Sheet at 30 September 1989

	£	£
Fixed assets		
Leasehold shop at cost	12,100	
Less accumulated depreciation	9,360	
		2,740
Shop equipment at cost	19,634	
Less accumulated depreciation	13,007	
		6,627
		9,367
Current assets		
Stock	1,240	
Debtors	241	
Prepayments	824	
Cash at bank	6,912	
Deposit account (W1)	835	
	10,052	
Current liabilities		
Creditors	786	
Accruals	210	
	996	
Working capital		9,056
		18,423
Financed by:		
Capital		
Balance at 1 October 1988		17,518
Add profit for year		7,452
Less drawings (W2)		(6,547)
		18,423

Workings

W1. 6,412 (opening balance) + 500 (transfer from current account) = 6,912.

Note that the interest has been paid into the current account, and so does not have to be entered again.

W2. 1,047 (from current account) + 5,500 (takings not banked) = 6,547.

Question 5

Tower
Trading and profit and loss account for the year to December 1991

	£000	£000
Sales (800 - 16)		784
Opening stock	125	
Purchases (620 - 3 - 5)	612	
Less Closing stock (136 - 6)	130	
		607
Gross profit		177
Interest	6	
Depreciation 40% x {(25 + 5) - 10}	8	
Rates (16 - 2)	14	
Bank interest (1 + 1)	2	
Bank charges (2 + 2)	4	
Wages	31	
Delivery expenses	7	
Heat, etc.	9	
General expenses	21	
Bad debts	4	
Provision for bad debts	9	
		115
Net profit		62

Balance sheet at 31 December 1991

	£000	£000
Fixed Assets		
Premises		108
Fixtures and fittings at cost (25 + 5)	30	
Less accumulated stock	18	
		12
		120
Current assets		
Stock	130	
Debtors (64-16-4-9)	35	
Prepayment	2	
Current assets	167	
Current Liabilities		
Creditors	38	
Bank	7	
Interest due	6	
Bank interest accrued	2	
Bank charges accrued	1	
Current liabilities	54	
Working capital		113
		233
Loan		50
		183
Opening capital		148
Profit		62
Drawings		-27
Closing capital		183

Question 6

To answer this question requires an appreciation of the difference between variable costs and fixed costs. Variable costs are those that change in direct proportion to output, so that, for example, a 10% increase in output causes variable costs to rise by 10%. Fixed costs do not vary with activity, but above their maximum capacity, an additional set of fixed costs must be incurred. In this question, the variable and fixed costs are labelled as such, with the exception of depreciation, which is a fixed cost.

The entries in the profit and loss accounts for the three years are found by multiplying the number of units by the amount per unit for revenue, materials and labour and then including the fixed costs, which do not change from year to year.

The break even point is where neither a profit nor a loss is made. As the cost structure does not change over the years, neither does the break even point.

The answer to part (d) depends on the fact that to produce a relatively small extra amount of Aristo requires the purchase of a new set of fixed assets. The extra sales of 10,000 units do not generate a contribution large enough to cover the additional depreciation.

(a)

Aristo

	1991 £000	1992 £000	1993 £000
Sales	270	360	450
Material	54	72	90
Labour	66	88	110
Depreciation	90	90	90
Fixed costs	100	100	100
	310	350	390
Profit (loss)	(40)	10	60

Tottle

	1991 £000	1992 £000	1993 £000
Sales	190	285	380
Material	32	48	64
Labour	18	27	36
Depreciation	20	20	20
Fixed costs	92	92	92
	162	187	212
Profit (loss)	28	98	168

(b)

	Aristo	Tottle
Selling price per unit	9.0	9.5
Variable cost per unit	4.0	2.5
Contribution per unit	5.0	7.0
Fixed costs	190,000	112,000
Break even point	190,000 / 5.0	112,000 / 7.0
	= 38,000 units	= 16,000 units

(c) In each of the three years Tottle makes higher profits then Aristo. It has a higher contribution and lower fixed costs; these give it a much lower break even point. The number of units sold is not as important as the amount of profit generated, and this is a function of contribution and fixed costs.

(d) Buy from Hume. Each unit bought and sold would produce a contribution of 9-8 =1. As there are no additional fixed costs to meet, sales of 10,000 units would add 10,000 to profit.

Buy additional plant. The contribution from each unit is 5, but additional fixed costs, in the form of depreciation have to be met. Additional depreciation would be 90,000, and so extra sales of 10,000 units would give a loss of 40,000.

Question 7

The first stage in answering this question involves the calculation of the partnership's trading profit. To do this, the profit in the draft accounts has to be adjusted for depreciation, rates and the bad debt and drawings added back, as the profit to be divided between the partners must be found before any amounts have been paid to the partners. Note that the depreciation of the car and the bad debt reduce profit while the rates are a prepayment and so add to the profit for the year. The premises and car introduced by Opal are entered in the balance sheets as assets, depreciated as necessary and represent Opal's capital.

When preparing partnership accounts, it is necessary to keep a separate record of the relationship between the firm and each individual partner. In this case, the partners have also decided to maintain separate capital and current accounts. The result of this can be seen in the balance sheet, where the capital accounts are recorded separately from the current accounts, and there is a current account for each partner.

Part (c) of the question is a straightforward test of knowledge, which most students answered correctly. However, it was clear that there were a number of guesses involving the ratio of capital invested, and these attracted no marks.

(a)

		£	£
Profit per draft accounts			41,000
Depreciation of car			-2,000
Rates			6,000
Bad debt			-1,000
Add back drawings			<u>38,000</u>
			82,000
Interest:	Ruby	7,000	
	Pearl	5,000	
	Opal	4,000	
Salary:	Ruby	9,000	
	Pearl	6,000	
	Opal	<u>12,000</u>	
			<u>43,000</u>
Residue: 1/3 each = 13,000			39,000

(b)

	£	£	£	£
Fixed assets at cost				150,000
Less accumulated depreciation				22,000
				128,000
Stock			50,000	
Trade debtors			59,000	
Prepayment			6,000	
Cash			1,000	
			116,000	
Trade creditors			40,000	
				76,000
				204,000

Financed by:
Capital introduced:
Ruby				70,000
Pearl				50,000
Opal				40,000
				160,000

Current accounts:	Ruby	Pearl	Opal	
Profit residue	13,000	13,000	13,000	
Interest	7,000	5,000	4,000	
Salary	9,000	6,000	12,000	
	29,000	24,000	29,000	
Drawings	10,000	15,000	13,000	
	19,000	9,000	16,000	44,000
				204,000

(c) If the partners do not agree to the contrary, the profit would be split equally between the partners (Partnership Act 1890). The profit would be calculated before any other payments (interest, salaries, etc.) had been paid to the partners.

Question 8

(a) The cash account consists of two columns of figures, one of inflows of cash and the other of outflows. The inflows are known as debits, and the outflows as credits. The difference between the two lists is the balance; in this case the inflows exceed the outflows and so there is a debit balance. It was not necessary to present answers in the form of a T account as given below, but there must be some consistent way of distinguishing between the two different types of flow.

Cash account

Debit		£	Credit	£
Capital		7,000	Van	6,000
Sales		15,000	Ladders	550
			Sign writing	450
			Sundry costs	1,025
			Motor expenses	1,500
			Casual labour	2,500
			Drawings	9,000
			Balance c/d	975
		22,000		22,000
Balance b/d		975		

(b) The bank reconciliation starts with the cash account balance and adjusts it for items which do not appear both in the cash book and on the bank statement. There is no need to prepare another full cash account, as this was done in answer to part (a), or as many students did, a copy of the bank statement, since details of the differences are provided in the question. The reconciliation is:

	£
Cash account balance	975
Plus uncleared cheque	890
Less outstanding lodgements	(50)
Balance on bank statement	1,815

(c) The cost of buying the van and having a sign painted on it are both capital expenditure, and should be included in the cost of the van to be written off over its life. The value of the van at the end of the first years trading is given and so the depreciation charge for the year can be found:

	£
Cost of van	6,000
Add sign writing	450
	6,450
Less value at end of year	5,310
Depreciation for year	1,140

The total amount to be written off over the life of the van is:

Cost	6,450
Less residual value	750
	5,700

Using the straight-line basis, this gives an annual charge of:

5,700/5 = 1,140, i.e. the same value as that found above.

Alternatively, the depreciable amount could have been divided by the first year's charge to see if there was an identifiable relationship:

5,700/1,140 = 5, i.e. the life of the van.

Therefore, a straight-line depreciation policy is being used to write off the net value of the van over its five-year life.

(d) The main errors in this part were to omit all the adjustments needed to convert cash flows to trading flows. Closing debtors must be added to sales and accruals added to expenses; the debtors and accruals are then included in the balance sheet as current assets and current liabilities respectively. These adjustments are clearly shown in the following solution to this part of the question. Again, note the need to show workings so that credit can be given wherever possible.

In the balance sheet, the values included for cash and profit should be consistent with those calculated elsewhere.

Matrix
Profit and loss account for the year to 30 June 1991

Sales (15,000 + 750)		15,750
Materials (1,025 + 75)	1,100	
Motor expenses (1,500 + 85)	1,585	
Labour	2,500	
Depreciation:		
Ladders (550 - 405)	145	
Van (6,450 - 5,310)	1,140	
		6,470
Net profit		9,280

Matrix
Balance Sheet at 30 June 1991

	£	£
Fixed assets		
Van (6,450 - 1,140)		5,310
Ladders (550 - 145)		405
		5,715
Current assets		
Debtors	750	
Cash	975	
	1,725	
Current liabilities		
Accrued sundry materials	75	
Accrued motor expenses	85	
	160	
Working capital		1,565
		7,280
Financed by:		
Opening capital		7,000
Add profit for year		9,280
Less drawings		(9,000)
		7,280

Question 9

Students who did not know what the entity concept is could only achieve a maximum mark of 10 on this question, and it was noticeable that many answers did not even attempt part (a). This indicates either a lack of preparedness for the examination or poor ability to select which questions to answer. The need to ensure that all aspects of the requirements of questions are dealt with cannot be emphasised enough. Part (a) of this question involves a definition of the term entity concept, an explanation of its effect on the preparation of accounting reports, and the use of provided information to illustrate its impact. Many students were of the opinion that the entity concept had legal backing in all cases; this in fact only applies in the case of limited companies, whereas the concept is applied to the accounting reports of all types of firm, including sole traders and partnerships. A correct answer would be as follows.

(a) The entity concept is the assumption, for accounting purposes, that the business has an existence separate and distinct from its owners, managers, or any other individual with whom it comes into contact within the course of its activities. This division is legally recognised in the case of limited companies. The consequence is that accounting reports are prepared from the point of view of the entity and so it can record its relationship with its owners.

Relating this to Sutol & Co., only the transactions affecting the firm are recorded in its books:

1 Ignore the personal account; record capital introduced.

2 Record the van; ignore the car.

3 The house and its values are ignored; any overdraft incurred by the business is recorded.

4 Record the loan to the business and its interest.

5 Record the additional capital introduced.

6 Record the drawings as they are a transaction between the owner and the firm.

(b) The balance sheet of the firm should contain only those items relating to the business entity. Providing this rule is applied, the preparation of the balance sheet is straightforward. Many students tried to construct a profit and loss account, but this is both impossible, based on the information provided, and unnecessary. The fact that a balance sheet balances, enables the profit for the year to be found as a balancing figure, providing all the other entries have been made correctly. A knowledge of what should be included in a standard balance sheet and its layout is of great help in answering this part of the question.

Sutol & Co
Balance sheet at 31 December 1991

	£	£
Fixed assets		6,000
Stock	3,300	
Debtors	2,500	
Prepayment	260	
	6,060	
Creditors	1,125	
Overdraft	2,700	
Electricity	70	
Bank interest	110	
Loan interest	120	
	4,125	
		1,935
Loan		7,935
		4,000
		3,935
Opening capital		10,000
Capital introduced		1,000
		11,000
Profit (balancing figure)		7,935
		18,935
Drawings		15,000
		3,935

Question 10

(a)

Cash-flow forecast

Cash in	Jul	Aug	Sep	Oct	Nov	Dec
Sales cash	130	130	150	225	250	300
Credit	160	130	130	150	225	250
Debenture issue	400					
	690	260	280	375	475	550
Cash out						
Purchases	160	130	130	150	225	250
Stock increase					50	40
Wages	90	90	90	135	135	135
Expenses	26	26	26	39	39	39
Fixed assets		475				
Advertising				50	35	15
	276	721	296	359	464	464
Opening balance	5	419	(42)	(58)	(42)	(31)
Cash in	690	260	280	375	475	550
Cash out	276	721	296	359	464	464
Closing balance	419	(42)	(58)	(42)	(31)	55

(b) The proposed expansion envisages sales increasing by about 230% over six months; this is very optimistic. The company is committed to significant payments and increases in costs, but the increase in sales to match these cannot be guaranteed.

The anticipated working capital position will be (accrued debenture interest could also be included):

	£
Stock	220
Debtors	300
Cash	55
	575
Creditors (300 + 20)	320
Working capital	255

This is healthy, with a ratio of 1.8:1. If sales do not meet expectations, the cash and debtors figures will be lower, but so should the creditors figure. The cash position, but not the overall working capital, will also be affected by whether the ratio of cash to credit sales remains the same.

On the whole, students answered this question quite well, the main areas of weakness being:

- Not including the opening cash flows in July for the debtors and creditors in the balance sheet at 30 June 1994.

- Not retarding the credit sales and purchases by one month, especially in the case of the stock increases.

- Doubling the cost of wages and salaries and general expenses in October instead of adding 50% to the previous figure.

- Restricting the discussion in part (b) to cash; the requirement is to examine working capital.

- Accepting that the forecast increase in activity will be achieved.

- In part (b) dealing with only a single aspect; the requirement has two parts: comment on the proposed expansion and the working capital position.

5 Summary

5.1 In this Unit you have worked some past questions and hopefully had an insight into the way the examiner works. You should now do some thorough revision before attempting the final tutor marked assignment, a mock exam.

Unit 1

Answers to self-assessment questions

1. A balance sheet shows the assets and liabilities of a business, i.e. what the business owns and what is owed to the business, together with what it owes to the owners, suppliers and others.

2. Current assets are kept for less than one year in the business and consist of items used day to day. Fixed assets are purchased by the business with the object of keeping them for longer than a year. They are not intended for resale.

3. Long-term liabilities represent items that the business is going to own for more than a year, such as long-term loans. Current liabilities represent short-term commitments.

4. (a) Debtors represent the sums owing from customers who have been supplied goods and services on credit.

    (b) Creditors represent the sums owed to suppliers for goods and services supplied on credit.

    (c) Drawings comprise money and goods taken from the business by the owners in anticipation of profit.

    (d) Capital comprises the money and assets provided by the owner(s) to the business to start it and which may be added later to assist expansion.

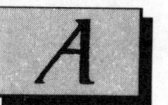

5. The completed table should look like this:

	Assets		Liabilities		Capital
(a)	50,000	=	40,000	+	10,000
(b)	80,000	=	65,000	+	15,000
(c)	60,000	=	15,000	+	45,000

6. The correct order for the current assets is most fixed to most liquid, therefore:

    Stock, Debtors, Bank, Cash.

7. A current liability is an amount outstanding for less than a year that is owed by the business, e.g. bank overdraft, trade creditor.

8. The correct heading for a balance sheet is 'as at...' followed by the date. The heading should indicate the name of the business it represents.

9. Debtors appear as assets in the balance sheet.

10   You balance sheet should look like this:

Your Business
Balance sheet as at 31 December 19XX

	£	£
Fixed assets		
Premises		10,000
Equipment		2,000
		12,000
Current assets		
Stock	4,000	
Debtors	2,000	
Bank	500	
	6,500	
Current liabilities		
Creditors	2,000	
Working capital		4,500
		16,500
Capital		15,000
Net profit		3,000
		18,000
Drawings		1,500
		16,500

Unit 6

Answers to self-assessment questions

1. A partnership is a relationship which exists between persons carrying on a business in common with a view to profit.

2. The partnership agreement states:

    (a) the capital is to be contributed by each partner

    (b) how the profits and losses are to be divided

    (c) interest to be paid on partners' loans

    (d) partners' drawings

    (e) what is to happen if a partner leaves/retires from the firm and a new partner is to be bought in to retain the status quo.

3. The rules contained within the Partnership Act of 1890 are:

    (a) all profits and losses to be shared equally among the partners

    (b) no interest on capital is payable, or for conducting the business

    (c) partners are entitled to 5% interest on loans above the amount of capital

    (d) every partner is allowed to take part in the management of the business.

    (e) all existing partners need to agree to the inclusion of a new partner.

4. Partners charge interest on drawings and receive interest on capital as a way of rewarding partners who take less out of the business by way of drawings and contribute most by way of capital.

5. Partners have current and capital accounts to separate the day-to-day transactions from the initial capital injection.

6. Drawings represent money taken out of the partnership in anticipation of profit rather than a sharing of profits and are therefore shown in the current accounts of partners. The appropriation account shows how profits are shared.

8   51,450 less 45,000 = 6,450 loss.

9   Depreciation is disclosed in the profit and loss account as a charge or expense for the year.

10 In the balance sheet, the accumulated depreciation on fixed assets is deducted from the fixed asset cost.

Unit 5

Answers to self-assessment questions

1. Depreciation is a means of gradually reducing the balance sheet value of a fixed asset in the account to represent the way that the fixed assets wear out over time.

2. Depreciation is charged on fixed assets to match the use of a fixed asset against the time periods during which it is used.

3. Straight-line and reducing balance method.

4. $$\frac{\text{Cost less resale or scrap value}}{\text{Expected life}}$$

5. $1 - n\sqrt{\dfrac{s}{c}}$

   where n = number of years $\quad s$ = scrap value $\quad c$ = cost

6. The following are estimates:
   - scrap value
   - number of years of life.

7. The depreciation charge for the next three years is:

   Year 1

Cost of fixed assets	150,000
30% of 150,000	45,000
	105,000

   Year 2

Book value	105,000
30% of 105,000	31,500
	73,500

   Year 3

Book value	73,500
30% of 73,500	22,050
	51,450

Unit 4

Answers to self-assessment questions

1. A prepayment is a payment in advance for a period beyond the current accounting period. It is shown on the balance sheet in the current assets.

2. The amount of the prepayment is deducted from the entire cash payment made in the profit and loss account so that the amount in the account covers the expense for the accounting period only.

3. An accrual is an amount owing at the end of the current accounting period for services provided. It is shown as a current liability on the balance sheet.

4. An accrual is added to the total cash payment made for the relevant expense in the profit and loss account so that the total expense incurred for the accounting period is reflected in the accounts.

5. The net profit could be erroneously increased or decreased by the incorrect treatment of accruals and prepayments.

6. A bad debt is created to reflect that a customer is very unlikely to pay the amount owed to the business for goods or services previously supplied on credit. The double entry treatment is:

    Dr   Bad debts account

    Cr   Debtor

7. A business has a provision for bad debts account to recognise the extent to which outstanding debtors might not pay up.

8. An increase in the provision for bad debts, will decrease the profit.

9. Bad debts and increases in provisions for bad debts appear as an expense in the profit and loss account. A decrease in provision for bad debts is a credit entry.

    No disclosure is needed for bad debts in the balance sheet. This is because any bad debts are not included in the debtors figure taken to the balance sheet. The provision for bad debts is deducted from the figure for outstanding debtors.

10. Adjustments are made in the accounts for accruals, prepayments, bad debts and provisions for bad debts to ensure that the trading, profit and loss account and balance sheet for the current accounting period include only income and expenditure incurred during the period, rather than before or after.

7   (a) Debit.

    (b) Credit.

    (c) Credit.

    (d) Debit.

8   An error of principle is where an entry is made in the account, e.g. wages debited to purchases.

9   An error of omission occurs where a transaction has been completely omitted from the accounts.

10 Drawings of stock are included in the accounts as follows:

    Dr   Drawings

    Cr   Purchases

Unit 3

Answers to self-assessment questions

1.

Transaction	Debit	Credit
Bought car for cash	Motor vehicles	Cash
Sold goods for cash	Cash	Sales
Paid wages by cheque	Wages	Bank
Bought goods from G. Jones	Purchases	G. Jones

2. In double entry bookkeeping, every debit entry in the accounts gives rise to an equal credit entry, illustrating the dual effect of transactions, for every purchaser, there is a seller, and so on.

3. Personal accounts identify individuals and firms with whom the business trades such as individual debtors and creditors. Nominal accounts refer to records of transactions which are not personal, such as rent, wages, purchases, and so on.

4. (a) Debited.

    (b) Credited.

    (c) Debited.

5.

Stock a/c

Dr		Cr	
Creditor	400		

Creditors a/c

Dr		Cr	
Cash	300	Stock	400

Cash a/c

Dr		Cr	
		Creditor	300

6. A trial balance is a list of debtors and creditors drawn up to prove the arithmetical accuracy of the double entry system and to act as an initial step before drawing up the final accounts.

8   Gross profit is calculated by preparing a trading account.

Trading account for the year ended...

	£	£	£
Sales			100,000
Opening stock		12,000	
Add purchases	66,000		
Less purchases returns	5,000	61,000	
		73,000	
Less closing stock		16,000	
Cost of goods sold			57,000
Gross profit			43,000

9   (a) Carriage outwards appears as an expense in the profit and loss account.

   (b) Carriage inwards is a cost of purchasing. It is added to Purchases in the trading account.

10 The net profit is calculated by drawing up a trading, profit and loss account.

Trading profit and loss account for the year ended...

	£	£	£
Sales			200,000
Less returns inwards			800
			199,200
Opening stock		10,000	
Add purchases	90,000		
Less returns out	1,000		
	89,000		
Add carriage in	600		
		89,600	
		99,600	
Less closing stock		8,000	
Cost of goods sold			
			91,600
Gross profit			107,600
Less expenses			
Carriage out		400	
Heating and lighting		1,200	
Rent and rates		2,400	
Salaries		9,000	
			13,000
Net profit			94,600

Unit 2

Answers to self-assessment questions

1. A trading account is a financial statement which shows the success of a business in buying and selling goods.

2. A profit and loss account comprises the income and expenses of a business over a period of time and is used to calculate the net profit, a measure of the success of operations.

3. The trading profit and loss account is headed:

    [Company name]

    Trading profit and loss account for the year ended [followed by the date].

    The balance sheet is headed:

    [Company name]

    Balance Sheet as at [followed by the date].

    This shows that the balance sheet is drawn up and comprises the balances on accounts on one specific day. The trading profit and loss account comprises the totals accumulate within the period measured.

4. (a) Gross profit = Sales - Cost of goods sold

    (b) Net profit = Gross profit - Operating Expenses

    (c) Net profit/loss is added to/deducted from the capital figure.

5. (a) Capital expenditure is the purchase of, or an addition in, value to a fixed asset.

    (b) Revenue expenditure is the purchase cost of items incurred in the normal course of business which do not add any value to the fixed assets.

6. Capital expenditure is reflected in the balance sheet because of the increase in value of the fixed assets.

    Revenue expenditure is reflected in the trading profit and loss account because the items purchased will in the main be used in the current accounting period.

7. Sales returns represent goods returned to the business from customers. Purchases returns represent goods returned by the business to suppliers.

Unit 7

Answers to self-assessment questions

1. A company is a separate legal entity governed by the Companies Acts.

2. Limited liability means that the liability of members in the event of liquidation is limited to the amount of the shareholdings. If a company cannot afford to pay its bills, members private assets are safe.

3. A dividend is an appropriation of profit which provides shareholders with a share of the profits earned by the company of which they are members or owners.

4. Reserves are an accumulation of profits from trading and sales of assets which can be invested in the general expansion of the company or used for specific expenditure.

5. A debenture is a company loan which may be secured or unsecured.

6. Equity is ordinary share capital or capital and reserves.

7. Bonus issues are shares created from the adjustment of reserves. Rights issues are new shares issued to shareholders for cash.

8. Ordinary shares usually have voting rights and take the greater risk in companies. Rates of dividend alter from one year to the next. Preference shares are usually issued with a fixed rate of dividend and without a right to vote in company meetings. They are a less risky form of investment for shareholders.

9. Corporation tax.

10. A provision is an amount put aside for a loss in value of assets and reflects the idea of prudent accounting. A reserve is money put aside for future investment in the business.

Unit 8

Answers to self-assessment questions

1. Incomplete records comprise any business records where only part of a transaction is included, i.e. anything other than conventional double entry.

2. Small businesses have little need for full records beyond the cash book and details of debtors and creditors. Keeping more extensive records is time-consuming.

3. The balance sheet equation is Assets = Capital + Liabilities or C = A − L.

4. The net profit is the difference between the capital of two years.

5. Purchases will be 10,000.

6. The sales figure is 42,000 + 12,000 - 15,000 = 39,000

7. The purchase figure is 79,000 + 27,000 - 12,000 = 94,000

8. Accrued rent due at the end of the current year would be added to the cash payment for rent made during the year and the accrued rent due at the start of the year would be deducted.

9. The insurance figure in the profit and loss account would be

    1,500 - 200 - 100 = 1,200.

10. Two from: depreciation, bad debts, provision for bad debts and other provisions.

Unit 9

Answers to self-assessment questions

1. FRS 1 is Financial Reporting Standard 1: Cash flow statements, which provides guidance on the content and presentation of these statements and requires them to be presented as part of the final accounts of many organisations.

2. Operating activities

   Returns on investment and financing

   Taxation

   Investing activities

   Financing.

3. Interest paid and received, dividends paid and received.

4. Corporation tax paid during the year.

5. The cash flow statement shows the cash inflow and outflow for the period covered and the way in which cash has been applied and obtained.

6. Changes in working capital are differences in short-term assets and liabilities other than changes in cash and bank balances.

7. Proposed dividends at the end of the year are added back to net profit in arriving at operating profit for the year. Proposed dividends at the end of last year and paid dividends during the year appear within returns on investment and financing.

8. Shares and loans are included in a cash flow statement as financing. Both shares and loans issued and redeemed and repaid appear under this heading.

9. Depreciation is added back to arrive at the figure for inflow or outflow from operating activities.

10. Adjustments for tax, dividends and any transfers to and from reserves would be made to recalculate profit.

Unit 10

Answers to self-assessment questions

1. A fixed cost is one that does not alter at different levels of activity. Variable costs alter directly in response to levels of activity.

2. A direct cost is directly related to the individual units of the business. Indirect cost are those costs not directly related to a single unit but are shared by several.

3. The following are both fixed costs and indirect costs:
   - Annual rent for factory and offices 10,000
   - Factory manager's salary 15,000 p.a.

   The following is a fixed cost and may be a direct or indirect cost:
   - Annual depreciation of manufacturing plant 6,000

   The decision depends on how closely linked the manufacturing plant is to a specific product.

   The following are both variable costs and direct costs:
   - Materials per unit 4.20
   - Direct wages per unit 5.50

4. Contribution = Sales Variable Costs

5. Contribution per unit:
   - Sales income per unit   7.00
   - Variable costs per unit   5.00
   - Contribution per unit   2.00

6. $$\text{Break even} = \frac{\text{Fixed Costs}}{\text{Contribution per unit}}$$

7. The break even point of a business identifies the point at which a business starts to make a profit on a product.

8. The margin of safety is the amount by which forecast sales exceed the break even point.

9. $$\text{Units sold} = \frac{\text{Fixed cost} + \text{Desired profit}}{\text{Contribution per unit}}$$

10   The break even point is:

$$\frac{\text{Fixed Costs}}{\text{Contribution per unit}} = \frac{300{,}000}{14.00 - 8.00} = 50{,}000 \text{ units}$$

The margin of safety is:
Break even point	50,000 units
Forecast sales	100,000 units
Margin of safety	50,000 units

Unit 11

Answers to self-assessment questions

1. Organisations plan for investment, expansion and to improve profits.

2. Budgets are short-term plans which contribute towards meeting longer-term objectives.

3. A budget variance is the difference between actual results and budget figures. For example, sales may be lower than expected. The reasons for the variance are investigated and action taken to correct anything adverse.

4. Cash flow forecasts provide a basis for planning and highlight the implications of trading decisions on the cash resources of an organisation.

5. Inflation means that income from sales and costs increase without a change in volume of activity. The adjustments need to be allowed for in budgets and forecasts.

6. Cash flow forecasts are concerned simply with inflows and outflows of cash in a business. Depreciation is a bookkeeping entry not involving cash movements.

7. Timing is important because if money flows out of a firm faster than it comes in, the business may become short of funds and be unable to pay bills when they arise. Temporary problems can be overcome by borrowing. In the long term, however, inflows must be greater than outflows of cash to ensure survival.

8. The following formula shows the change:

   Opening balance + inflows - outflows = closing balance.

9. This occurs when businesses sell goods on credit. Customers are given a certain period of time to pay for the goods they bought, typically a month.

10. Increased sales means more income so inflows will increase as will the closing balance. And as more goods are being sold, purchases must be made to replace the goods sold, outflows will also increase to some extent. For example, if sales increase by 1,000 as 100 extra goods are sold, purchases may increase by 500 as the business buys another 100 units from suppliers.

Unit 12

Answers to self-assessment questions

1. Budgets are estimates of expected activity relating to specific areas of business such as sales, production and cash movements.

2. Cash flow forecasts are projections of expected cash flows over a period of time. Management and lending institutions are likely to be interested in them as a way of calculating needs for borrowing and indications of when borrowing will be repaid. In addition, excess cash can be invested and a cash flow forecast will indicate when surplus cash is available.

3. Profit is calculated with reference to accruals and other adjustments. Cash is more concrete and measures receipts and payments when they take place.

4. Depreciation is not included in the cash flow forecast as it is not a cash movement but an adjustment to profit.

5. The timings of cash received and paid are important to ensure that the forecast balances in a cash budget are likely to be accurate.

6. The length of credit taken and given influence when cash is received from customers and paid to suppliers.

7. Actual figures can be monitored against a cash budget to measure success in meeting repayments of overdrafts and loans.

8. In a seasonal business such as a firework manufacturer, there will be periods when the business has plenty of cash, after sales of fireworks. And, during the manufacturing process, cash will flow out.

9. In a cash budget both capital and revenue expenditure is brought in. This is because the cash budget measures cash and not profits.

10. Two cash inflows are sales income and loans received.

Unit 13

Answers to self-assessment questions

1. Accruals, consistency, going concern, prudence.

2. Accounting bases and principles.

3. Stock should be valued prudently 'at the lower end of cost and net realisable value'.

4. Net realisable value means the estimated selling price less any further costs to be incurred, on completion of a product, e.g. advertising, selling and delivery costs.

5. The disclosure requirements for depreciation of fixed assets are:

    1. the depreciation method used

    2. the useful economic life

    3. the total depreciation for year

    4. the gross amount of depreciable assets and the related accumulated depreciation.

6. Purchased goodwill arises on the purchase of a business and represents the purchase price paid is over and above the cost of the net assets. Non-purchased goodwill can arise when a going concern is worth more than the fair values of its net assets but does not result from a purchase of the business. Non-purchased should not be disclosed in the accounts.

7. The optional treatments of goodwill contained in SSAP 22 are:

    - immediate write-off against reserves

    - amortise over its useful life (treat like depreciation). Useful life is decided when the goodwill comes into the business.

8. The objective of FRS 1 is for companies to show how they generated their money and what they spent it on.

9. The objective of FRS 3 aids users in understanding the performance achieved by a reporting entity in a period and to assist them in forming a basis for their assessment of future results and cash flows.

10. Ordinary activities are defined in FRS 3 as:

    'any activities undertaken by the reporting entity that are in the normal course of their business. Ordinary activities include the effects on the reporting entity of any event in the various environments in which it operates, including the political, regulatory, economic and geographical environments, irrespective of the frequency or unusual nature of the events'.

Unit 14

Answers to self-assessment questions

1. Bank reconciliation statements are drawn up to compare items in the cash book with the bank statement and identify errors and outstanding items.

2. Usually each time a bank statement is received.

3. Balance as per (adjusted) cash book and balance as per bank statement.

4. Bank reconciliation statement as at [date].

5. Because there will be items in the cash book which have yet to reach the bank statement and items in the bank statement not yet recorded in the cash book. There may also be errors in either financial statement.

6. Bank interest, charges, standing orders and direct debits.

7. Cheques issued but not yet presented and credit items paid into another branch, a nightsafe and so on.

8. Bank charges appear on the credit side of the business cash book. Charges are regarded as a debit entry in the bank and this reflects the fact that the bank keeps the records of its customers as a mirror image of the business records. This arises from the application of double entry principles.

9. A bank overdraft is a liability in the books of the business.

10. The bank reconciliation provides a way of ascertaining the correct bank balance to be included in the balance sheet and highlights all receipts and payments to be included in the calculations of revenue items for the trading profit and loss account.

Unit 15

Answers to self-assessment questions

1. Gross profit ratio and net profit ratio are both profitability ratios.

2. The equation for calculating return on capital employed is:

   $$\frac{\text{Net profit before tax and interest}}{\text{Capital employed}}$$

3. The formula for calculating the working capital ratio is:

   $$\frac{\text{Current assets}}{\text{Current liabilities}}$$

4. Stock is included as part of the total current assets in the working capital ratio but excluded when calculating the liquidity ratio.

5. The ratio of collection time for debtors measures the pay-up time of customers who buy on credit.

6. The speed at which stock is used in the business is measured by rate of stock turnover.

7. The formula for gearing is:

   $$\frac{\text{Long-term liabilities + preference shares} \times 100}{\text{Equity}}$$

8. Interest cover indicates how many times interest can be covered by earnings. The higher the rate of cover, the greater likelihood that the banker will have interest on borrowing paid. Therefore a business with a high interest cover is less risky than one with a low level of cover.

9. Ratio analysis does not give an indication of the type of business and does not automatically take differences in accounting policies between organisations into account.

10. Ratios are a useful tool in the interpretation of accounts. They provide a straightforward way of comparing organisations or one organisation over time with single figures.

Unit 16

Answers to self-assessment questions

1. Net realisable value is the selling price of goods less the expenses associated with selling.

2. FIFO, LIFO and AVCO are all methods of valuing stock.

3. SSAP 9: Stocks and work-in-progress.

4. A direct cost is one directly attributable to the manufacturing process.

5. Raw materials and work-in-progress.

6. An indirect cost.

7. Direct materials and direct wages.

8. Factory indirect costs.

9. The cost of production.

10. Some costs are apportioned to the different accounts to reflect the usage of these expenses with the factory and in other parts of the business.

Index

Introduction

Index entries refer first to unit numbers and secondly to the page number within the unit. Alphabetical arrangement is word-by-word, where a group of letters followed by a space is filed before the same group of letters followed by a letter, e.g. 'Bank statements' will appear before 'Bankers'. In determining alphabetical arrangement, initial articles and small prepositions are ignored.

A

Accounting bases, 13:3

Accounting concepts
SSAP2, 13:1-3

Accounting policies
SSAP2, 13:1-3

Accounting standards, 13:1-10
see also Financial Reporting Standards; Statements of Standard Accounting Practice

Accruals, 4:1-2
accounting treatment, 4:3-9
definition, 4:12

Accruals concept, 13:2

Appropriation account
company accounts, 7:5, 11
partnership accounts, 6:2-5

Assets, 1:1-2
definition, 1:5
see also Current assets; Fixed assets

Auditors fees
accounting treatment, 7:9

Auditors report, 13:4

Authorised share capital, 7:3

Bad debts, 4:10-17
    provision, 4:12-17
    prudence concept, 13:2

Balance sheet, 1:1-18
    accounting treatment of accruals and prepayments, 4:9
    accounting treatment of bad debts, 4:15-17
    building, 1:3
    capital, 1:8
    capital expenditure, 2:7-8
    company accounts, 7:12
    creditors, 1:4
    debtors, 1:6-7
    depreciation, 5:5-8
    from incomplete records, 8:4-5, 12-13, 14
    horizontal style, 1:2
    movement of assets and liabilities, 1:9-13
    partnership accounts, 6:5-8, 9
    presentation, 1:2, 14-15
    revenue expenditure, 2:8
    vertical style, 1:14-15
    worked example, 3:16, 21

Balance sheet equation, 8:2

Bank reconciliation, 14:1-7

Banks loans
    use of cash flow forecasts, 12:7-8

Bonus issue, 7:13

Bookkeeping
    worked example, 3:12-16
    see also Double entry bookkeeping

Break even analysis, 10:4-8

Budget variance
    definition, 11:1

Budgets, 11:1-2

B

C

Capital, 1:8

Capital accounts
    interest, 6:10-16
    partnership, 6:5

Capital adequacy
    ratio analysis, 15:6

Capital expenditure, 2:7
    balance sheet treatment, 2:7-8

Carriage inwards and carriage outwards, 2:8
    accounts treatment, 2:9

Cash account, 3:5

Cash book
    reconcilation with bank statement, 14:1-7

Cash flow forecasts, 11:1-13, 12:1-9
    definition, 11:2
    effect of giving credit, 12:2-6
    effect of taking credit, 12:1-2
    how to draw up, 11:4-11
    inflation, 11:3, 11
    purpose, 11:2-3
    used to assess a bank loan or overdraft, 12:7-8

Cash flow management
    timing of inflows and outflows of cash, 11:8-9

Cash flow statements, 9:1-16
    changes in working capital, 9:2-3
    corporation tax, 9:2, 4
    depreciation, 9:2
    dividends, 9:2, 4
    fixed assets, 9:2, 4
    information needed to draw up, 9:6-9
    interest, 9:2
    layout, 9:5
    limited companies, 9:9-14
    loans, 9:2, 4
    requirements of FRS 1, 9:1-4, 13:6-7
    shares, 9:2, 4
    standard headings, 9:2

Changing prices *see* **Inflation**

Companies
    definition, 7:1
    limited, 7:1-14
    registration, 7:1
    types, 7:1

Companies Acts 1985 and 1989, 7:1

Companies House, 7:1

Company accounts, 7:1-14
    appropriation account, 7:5, 11
    auditors fees, 7:9
    balance sheet, 7:12
    corporation tax, 7:2
    current liabilities, 7:9
    debentures, 7:8-9
    directors remuneration, 7:9
    dividends, 7:2, 12
    long-term liabilities, 7:8
    provisions, 7:2
    reserves, 7:2-4
    turnover, 7:2

Consistency concept, 13:2, 8

Contribution
    definition, 10:4-5

Contribution costing, 10:8

Corporation tax, 7:2
    cash flow statements, 9:2, 4

Costing, 10:1-10
    break even analysis, 10:4-5
    contribution costing, 10:8
    direct and indirect costs, 10:3-4, 16:7-8
    fixed costs, 10:1-3
    labour, 16:8
    manufacturing costs, 16:8
    margin of safety, 10:5-8
    production costs, 16:8
    raw materials, 16:8
    stock, 16:2
    target profit calculation, 10:8-9
    variable costs, 10:1-3, 16:8

Creditors
    balance sheet, 1:4
    ratio analysis, 15:5

Creditors ledger, 3:7

Current accounts (partnerships), 6:5-9
    drawings, 6:5, 10-14

Current assets, 1:7

Current liabilities, 1:8
    outstanding interest and dividends, 7:9

Debentures, 7:8

Debtors
    balance sheet, 1:6-7
    ratio analysis, 15:5
    see also Bad debts

Debtors ledger, 3:7

Depreciation, 5:1-14
    accounting treatment, 5:5-8, 13:5-6
    cash flow statements, 9:2
    definition, 5:1
    fixed assets, 5:2, 8-9, 13:6
    methods, 5:2-5
    reducing balance method, 5:2-4
    SSAP 12, 13:5-6
    straight-line method, 5:2-4

Depreciation charge
    annual, 5:8
    monthly, 5:12

Direct costs, 10:3-4, 16:7-8

Directors remuneration
    accounting treatment, 7:9

Disposal of fixed assets
    accounting treatment, 5:8-12

Dividends, 7:2, 12
    cash flow statements, 9:2, 4

Double entry bookkeeping, 3:1-3
    errors, 3:8
    ledger accounts, 3:3-7
    trial balance, 3:7-10

Drawings, 1:8
    accounting treatment, 3:12
    partnership accounts, 6:5, 10-14

E

Equity
    definition, 7:12

Error of omission, 3:8

Error of principle, 3:8

Exceptional items
    definition, 13:7

Extraordinary activities
    definition, 13:7

Fair value
   definition, 13:6

FIFO, 16:3-5

Financial Reporting Standards
   FRS 1 Cash flow statements, 9:1-4, 13:6-7
   FRS 3 Reporting financial performance, 13:7-8

First in first out, 16:3-5

Fixed assets, 1:7
   cash flow statements, 9:2, 4
   depreciation, 5:2, 8-9
   disclosure requirements for depreciation, 13:6
   disposal, 5:8-12

Fixed costs, 10:1-3

Forecasting, 11:2
   see also Cash flow forecasts

FRS *see* **Financial Reporting Standards**

G

Gearing
  ratio analysis, 15:6

General reserves, 7:8

Going concern concept, 13:2

Goodwill
  definitions, 13:6
  partnership, 6:14-16
  purchased and non-purchased, 13:6
  SSAP22, 13:6

Gross profit, 2:1-3

Gross profit ratio, 15:1, 3

Incomplete records, 8:1-16
    definition, 8:1
    drawing up accounts from, 8:2-15
    profit element, 8:10-11

Indirect costs, 10:3-4, 16:7-8

Inflation
    cash flow forecast, 11:3, 11

Interest
    cash flow statements, 9:2
    debentures, 7:8-9
    partnership accounts, 6:10-16

Interest cover
    ratio analysis, 15:6

Issued share capital, 7:3

L

Labour costs, 16:8

Last in first out, 16:3-5

Ledger accounts, 3:3-7
    worked example, 3:13-15, 19-20

Liabilities, 1:1-2
    current, 1:8, 7:9
    definition, 1:5
    long-term, 1:8, 7:8

LIFO, 16:3-5

Limited companies, 7:1
    accounts *see* Company accounts
    cash flow statements, 9:9-14

Liquidity ratio, 15:3-5

Loans
    cash flow statements, 9:2, 4
    see also Debentures

Long-term assets see Fixed assets

Long-term liabilities, 1:8
    company accounts, 7:8

Manufacturing accounts, 16:7-15

M

N

Net profit, 2:3-5

Net profit ratio, 15:2, 3

Net realisable value, 13:5
   stock, 16:2-3

Nominal accounts, 3:7

Ordinary activities
definition, 13:7

Ordinary shares, 7:3, 12

Overdrafts
use of cash flow forecasts, 12:7-8

P

Partnership accounts, 6:1-18
    appropriation account, 6:2-5
    balance sheet, 6:5-8, 9
    current accounts, 6:5-9
    drawings, 6:5, 10-14
    interest, 6:10-16

Partnership Act 1890, 6:1
    rules on the partnership agreement, 6:2

Partnership agreement, 6:2

Partnerships
    admission of a partner, 6:14-16
    capital accounts, 6:5, 10
    definition, 6:1-2
    goodwill, 6:14-16
    retirement of a partner, 6:14-16

Performance measurement
    ratio analysis, 15:1-13

Personal accounts, 3:7

Planning, 11:1
    see also Budgets; Cash flow forecasts

Preference shares, 7:3
    cumulative, 7:13
    non-cumulative, 7:12

Prepayments, 4:2
    accounting treatment, 4:3-9, 13:2
    definition, 4:12

Prime cost, 16:7-8

Prior year adjustments
    definition, 13:7

Private limited companies, 7:1

Production costs, 16:8

Profit and loss account
    accounting treatment of accruals and prepayments, 4:3-6
    auditors fees, 7:9
    carriage outwards, 2:9
    definition, 2:1
    depreciation, 5:5
    directors remuneration, 7:9
    format, 13:8
    provision for bad debts, 4:13-15
    revenue expenditure, 2:8

Provisions, 7:2
    bad debts, 4:12-17
    depreciation, 5:8

Prudence concept, 13:2

Public limited companies (PLCs), 7:1

Purchase ledger, 3:7

Purchase returns *see* **Returns outwards**

Purchased goodwill
    definition, 13:6

Purchases
    accounting treatment, 3:11

Ratio analysis, 15:1-13
    collection time of debtors and creditors, 15:5
    gearing, 15:6
    gross profit ratio, 15:1, 3
    interest cover, 15:6
    limitations, 15:12
    liquidity ratio, 15:3-5
    net profit ratio, 15:2, 3
    quick ratio, 15:3-5
    rate of stock turnover, 15:5
    return on capital employed, 15:2-3
    working capital ratio, 15:3-5

Raw materials
    costing, 16:8

Reserves, 7:2-4
    general, 7:8
    revaluation, 7:3, 7-8
    share premium, 7:6-7

Return on capital employed (ROCE), 15:2-3

Returns inwards
    accounts treatment, 2:10-13
    definition, 2:9

Returns outwards
    accounts treatment, 2:10-13
    definition, 2:9

Revaluation reserves, 7:3, 7-8

Revenue expenditure
    accounting for, 2:8
    definition, 2:8

Rights issue, 7:13

Sales
    accounting treatment, 3:11

Sales ledger, 3:7

Sales returns *see* **Returns inwards**

Share capital, 7:3-4

Share premium account, 7:3, 7

Share premium reserves, 7:6-7

Shares
    bonus issue, 7:13
    cash flow statements, 9:2, 4
    nominal value, 7:3
    par value, 7:3
    rights issue, 7:13
    types, 7:12-13

SSAPs *see* **Statements of Standard Accounting Practice**

Statements of Standard Accounting Practice
    SSAP 2 Disclosure of accounting policies, 13:1-3
    SSAP 9 Stocks and work-in-progress, 13:3-5, 16:7
    SSAP 12 Depreciation, 13:5-6
    SSAP 22 Goodwill, 13:6

Stock, 3:11
    cost, 16:2
    method of assessing, 16:3
    net realisable value, 16:2-3
    ratio analysis, 15:5
    SSAP 9, 13:3-5, 16,:7
    valuation, 16:1-7
    work-in-progress, 13:3-5, 16:7

T

Trading account
    carriage inwards, 2:9
    definition, 2:1

Trading profit and loss account, 2:1-15
    accruals and prepayments, 4:6-9
    bad debts, 4:15-17
    carriage inwards and carriage outwards, 2:9
    depreciation, 5:6-7
    directors remuneration, 7:10-11
    from incomplete records, 8:6-8, 14
    returns inwards and returns outwards, 2:10-13
    worked example, 3:16, 21

Trial balance, 3:7-10
    errors, 3:8
    worked example, 3:15, 20

True and fair view, 13:4

Turnover, 7:2

Valuation of stock, 16:1-7

Variable costs, 10:1-3, 16:8

W

Weighted average cost (AVCO), 16:5-7

Work-in-progress (WIP), 13:3-5, 16:7
    accounting for, 16:9

Working capital, 1:8-9
    changes in, 9:2-3

Working capital ratio, 15:3-5